PIRACY IN THE PACIFIC

PIRACY IN THE PACIFIC

THE STORY OF THE NOTORIOUS
RORIQUE BROTHERS

By HENRI JACQUIER

Translated by June P. Wilson

Illustrated with Photographs and Maps

DODD, MEAD & COMPANY
NEW YORK

Library of Congress Cataloging in Publication Data

Jacquier, Henri, 1907-
    Piracy in the Pacific.

    Translation of Piraterie dans le Pacifique.
    1. Rorique, Alexandre, 1854-1898. 2. Rorique, Joseph, 1865-1929? 3. Pirates—Society Islands. 4. Society Islands—History. I. Title.
    D4870.J3313   364.1'35 [B]   75-30661
    ISBN 0-396-07276-3

PREFACE

Such amazing things happen in this world that even if an author were able to conceive them, he would hesitate to use them for fear of seeming to stretch the truth.

Yet this is precisely what this author faced when he started to piece together the strange saga of the Rorique brothers which so enthralled the French and Belgian public at the end of the nineteenth century. To a population living dull lives under the leaden skies of Northern Europe, its locale, the odd cast of characters, and the nature of the crimes—piracy and murder—satisfied a craving for romantic derring-do in faraway places. Tahiti conjured up the mysterious beauty of the South Pacific islands, with their "noble savages," Gauguin's bare-breasted Polynesian beauties, the exploits of Cook, Bougainville and Robert Louis Stevenson, and the anonymous mariners in primitive sailing vessels who shuttled between the archipelagos with their exotic cargoes of mother-of-pearl, copra, sea slugs, sandalwood, spices and birds' nests. The personages in the drama were equally fantastic: two handsome brothers of mysterious origins who seemed to be the living embodiments of Dr. Jekyll and Mr. Hyde —Stevenson's book had appeared just five years earlier. Then, there was also the curious alliance between Europeans and natives forging viable commercial bonds between islands where only missionaries and adventurers had previously ventured.

When the trial was transferred to the Naval Jurisdiction in Brest, it traded an enchanted setting worthy of Prospero for the embattled political climate of the Third Republic caught up in the divisive antagonisms of the Panama Canal scandal and most particularly *l'Affaire Dreyfus*. It is not surprising that the same list of notable men and women involved in the Dreyfus case were also embroiled in the vagaries of the Rorique case: Sadi Carnot, President of the French Republic; Gabriel Hanotaux, Minister for Foreign Affairs; Félix Faure, Minister of the Navy; Georges Clemenceau, the "Tiger" of World War I; Emile Zola; Jules Verne, who used the subject in his book, *Les Frères Kipp*; Séverine, the famous suffragette and journalist; the American dancer Loïe Fuller; up to and including Leopold II, the King of the Belgians.

As a Breton by birth and Tahitian by adoption, I was naturally drawn to the Rorique saga. I had first heard about it from an old naval officer in Brest in 1931 where I was a young officer in the Naval Health Service. Two years later, I found myself in Tahiti where I came to know several people who had known the brothers. One of these, a Creole born in Papeete named Alexander Drollet, had an extraordinarily clear memory of the events. It was he who furnished the photographs of the brothers following page 112. Meanwhile, I had read *Les*

Frères Roriques by René La Bruyère, a former Navy
Commissioner stationed in Tahiti, whose book came out
in 1934. It was from these two men that I learned of the
brothers' activities in Papeete before they set sail on the
ill-fated *Niuroahiti*. Add to these the testimony of Vic-
torine Renvoyé, the daughter of Papeete's chief host at
whose restaurant the brothers often dined, and the bi-
monthly newspaper, *Le Messager de Tahiti*, whose publisher at the time was my wife's grandfather, Léonce Brault.
But by far the most telling source of information was the
voluminous dossier of the trial, preserved at the Service
Historique de la Marine, recently moved from the Place de
la Concorde in Paris to the Château de Vincennes just outside the capital.

I had decided I wanted to write the book just before
World War II. But when Brest was virtually destroyed by
a combination of American bombing and German demo-
lition, I assumed the dossier had disappeared in the rubble.
It wasn't until twenty years later that I learned, quite by
chance, that it had been transferred to Paris before the
outbreak of the war.

As for the old photographs of Papeete, these I found in
the Bibliotèque and Musée de la Société d'Etudes Océan-
iennes, of which I have been president for the past twenty
years. To my great joy, the photograph of the *Niuroahiti*
turned up in an album assembled by the then Director of
Postal Services, and had been turned over to an old gentleman serving as Director of Cadastre (or Land Bureau).
That picture made it possible to identify another photograph of the schooner found by a friend among the papers

of the Matthew Turner Shipyards which had built the ship near San Francisco.

I trust I do not need to protest the accuracy of the events described in my book. The facts needed no embellishment on my part. My only desire was to set them down as faithfully as possible, taking into full account the inevitable contradictions between the testimony of the accused and their accusers. At a time when means of communication are so many and so rapid, it is hard indeed to imagine how only eighty years ago, a ship could suddenly vanish from one region of the Pacific and reappear in another, bearing a fictitious name and falsified papers. But there are those who regret that what the great ocean has gained in security, it has lost for the romantic imagination.

ILLUSTRATIONS

[ix]

Illustrations

The steamer *Navua* moored in Papeete
San Francisco in 1917

MAPS

I

As NIGHT GAVE WAY to a pale dawn, details of the shoreline began to emerge: first, the long narrow ribbon of the coral beach, and parallel to it, row upon row of breakers beating against the reef, then the dark green curtain of vegetation, and finally, the silhouette of the mountains taking shape in the background.

Flying fish tinged with pink shot up out of the violet sea under the *Jessie Nicholls'* hull as the ship plied its modest course between the islands of the Cook archipelago. Pushed by a light northeast wind that came up with the day, it moved gently ahead, swaying in the vast swells of the South Pacific Ocean.

The trading schooner had left Penrhyn Island five days earlier. Called Tongareva in Polynesian, this large northern atoll was inhospitable, lacking almost everything including often fresh water. In addition to a cargo of mother-of-pearl and copra, the *Jessie Nicholls* had taken on a few natives and two white men—brothers who had supposedly been shipwrecked and had arrived at Penrhyn under somewhat mystifying circumstances. Their only possessions were their sailors' canvas dufflebags seized with drawstrings and wooden toggles. They were excellent sailors and had worked their passage by making repairs on the schooner, splicing the bolt rope in the foresail, testing the rigging, and punctiliously taking their turn at the helm. The captain noted with obvious satisfaction that despite their obscure background, they were clearly men with extensive experience of the sea.

Suddenly it was broad daylight. Just to the right of the bow they could see the anchorage and the wharf at Avarua, the main village on the island of Rarotonga. In June 1891, when this story began, the town had a thousand inhabitants and was the capital of a tiny kingdom under British protectorate, ruled by an aging and easygoing queen named Makea.

Unlike most of the Polynesian islands, Rarotonga had no lagoon, but this in no way diminished its charms. Less imposing than Tahiti, less romantic than Moorea or Bora-Bora, Rarotonga was more peaceful and its vegetation a little tamer than the untidy exuberance typical of Polynesia.

Avarua's anchorage was little more than an indentation in the fringe of reef. Most craft had to anchor out in the open sea. The shipwrecks lying at various points along the reef were eloquent testimony to the island's hazards.

The two sailors examined the approaches with apprehension, but this quickly changed to anticipation when their eyes took in the land beyond the beachside. After the many months they had spent on a barren atoll lost in the middle of the ocean, they were more than ready to appreciate the sight of these mountains, orange trees, waterfalls and streams.

Typical of all arrivals in the South Sea Islands, this one was cause for a joyous welcome, and the population crowded along the narrow wharf which had room only for the smallest boats. Among them were the local agent for the house of Delisle and Goodwin, who owned the *Jessie Nicholls*, and the British resident, the Honorable F. J. Moss, accompanied by a member of the local police, a very dignified native proudly wearing a constable's cap and a thick navy blue jersey in which he sweated copiously.

The officials' attention was drawn to the two foreigners who stood slightly apart. Did they have identification papers? No, they did not, having lost everything when their ship, the *General Brash*, went down in the narrows by the island of Jaluit. They did however have a certificate made out by the German resident in the Marshall Islands. It bore the Imperial Seal and related the circumstances of the shipwreck and the fact that the two brothers, Joseph and Alexander Rorick, born in Natal, South Africa, were the only survivors.

Alexander, the older of the two, expressed himself with ease in fluent English, although his accent was hard to place precisely. He was a magnificent specimen, six feet four inches tall, very thin, with steely blue eyes set in a face tanned by the sea and sun, dark brown hair and beard, and a deep vibrant voice—all of which gave him a hard-bitten and commanding presence. He was thirty-seven years old.

Joseph was ten years younger. Shorter, almost beardless, with a slight stoop and large, slightly bloodshot eyes, he

San Francisco

iian
Islands

Cook Is.　　Marquesas

Tuamotus

Tahiti　　Fakarava

rotonga
ook Is

Easter Is.

50°　　135°　　120°　　105°　　90°

V.W. Quinn

had a projecting tooth in his upper jaw which gave him a somewhat cynical air. But his expression was gentle and friendly, and he smiled at the girls who were peering at him with undisguised curiosity. Both men were dressed in patched but very clean coarse cotton pants and the usual cotton jerseys sold by Pacific traders. Their only finery consisted of two splendid wide-brimmed hats made in Manihiki from the white fiber of a special variety of pandanus, which their friends in Penrhyn had presented to them on their departure.

A native approached them and, in true Polynesian style, started to press them with questions about themselves, their family, their experiences. They answered slowly in Atiu, a Polynesian dialect which they had learned during their stay in the archipelago. The man invited them to his home. He lived nearby in a pretty oval-shaped hut by the edge of the sea. An enormous Barringtonia tree shaded the roof, and between its leathery green leaves, the sparkling waves could be seen exploding against the coral reef. Mama Raia, the mistress of the house, was a Polynesian of about forty with handsome features already tending toward fat. She welcomed the strangers as if they were long-lost friends and with no regard for the discrepancy in their ages, adopted them immediately. As their names were impossible to pronounce in Polynesian, Alexander became Teha, and Joseph, Tapeitau. Teha and Tapeitau soon discovered that the house contained several brothers and sisters, not to mention pecking chickens, a skinny dog and the familiar pig.

To earn their keep, the Roricks lost no time making themselves useful. At night, they pulled their gray cotton hammocks out of their duffles which they hung in a corner of the hut. When morning came, the hammocks were quickly taken down, rolled up and stowed away, exactly as in any well-ordered sailors' quarters. From the same duffles, they extracted a flute and an accordion. Thanks to these instruments, which they played with talent and verve, they made many friends; their family was ecstatic and their host's reputation soared to new heights.

They had yet to be accepted by Queen Makea and the resident British official. But the house of Delisle and Goodwin offered Joseph a position of warehouseman which consisted chiefly in clearing the imports that owed a ten percent tax to the royal treasury. Alexander was put in charge of the *Poe*, a small white schooner flying the Rarotonga flag which—like the Tahitian flag—consisted of three horizontal bands, red-white-red, with three stars on the white band. In short, everything pointed to a calm existence on an island blessed with peace and tranquillity.

Among the members of their new family was a pretty girl named Moe. Preferring to ignore the brother-sister relationship, they both courted her assiduously. One day, they rushed things a bit, Moe complained to Mama Raia, and she gave the brothers a stern lecture.

Among the Polynesian islands, Rarotonga had the reputation of being particularly virtuous. It had been converted to Christianity at the beginning of the century by the Reverend John Williams, one of the most intransigent ministers ever sent out by the London Missionary Society. A martyr to his faith, he was assassinated at Erromango, but his influence and presence remained undiminished. Stamped with a will of iron (which must have given even his directors in London pause), he had laid down the notorious "blue laws" which the resident Briton now prudently allowed to lapse. The Code ignored or condemned everything that did not lead directly to the soul's salvation. Rarotonga had no bar, sold no alcoholic beverages. Cohabitation between unmarried persons of different sexes was considered a crime and punishable as such. Meetings at night were forbidden. The moment darkness fell, anyone still abroad had to carry a lantern or torch; this prevented people from stumbling in the dark while permitting them to watch other people's comings and goings. Failure to heed this regulation, especially the deliberate extinguishing of the light, brought three days in prison. The Sabbath was rigorously observed, no fire could be lighted, and only cold foods prepared the night before were to be eaten.

On their first Sunday, the two brothers were solemnly conducted to church by their new family. They were paid the honor of sitting in front of the preacher's pulpit facing the faithful. The service included a sermon, readings and hymns, and lasted three hours. It resumed in a different form in the afternoon, and the evening was given over to discussion and religious songs.

Alexander visibly pined for life on board ship and the open sea, but Joseph seemed ready to live in Rarotonga forever, Moe's presence explaining in large part his desire to stay. But when Alexander decided to resume the life of adventure, his influence over his brother was such that Joseph was forced to give up whatever projects he was hatching.

They had been in Rarotonga about a month when they

woke up one morning to find a pretty schooner of California design flying the French flag, riding at anchor in Avarua's port. It was the *Papeete*, and it had just taken on a cargo of copra before returning to Tahiti. By a curious coincidence, both Wohler, the captain, and Nagel, his mate, were Germans. True, Wohler was a naturalized Frenchman so that he could sail under French colors. Neither had more than a smattering of French, and in talking to the Rorick brothers, they soon shifted to German. (The brothers seemed to know every language spoken in the Pacific.) Greatly impressed with their adventures, Wohler advised them to go to Tahiti where they were bound to find a vessel worthy of their skills and experience. And he added: "You will find Tahiti a very different place from Rarotonga!" Alexander made his decision then and there: they would both leave the next day on the *Papeete*. Before taking them on board, however, Wohler wanted to know a little more about their identities, chiefly to avoid any difficulties with the authorities in Tahiti. So the brothers produced their document, with the seal "Deutsche Reich" and the imperial eagle. The Germans were suitably impressed and all doubts were laid to rest.

All that remained for Alexander and Joseph was to pack their duffles. The parting proved difficult. The entire family came to the wharf, and Mama Raia wept as she draped the *heis* of tiare flowers around her adopted sons' necks. As the *Papeete* weighed anchor and hoisted its jib and foresail, the group crowding the end of the wharf raised its voice in a solemn chant: "Farewell, Teha! Farewell, Tapeitau! We will never see you again!"

Swallowing hard, the brothers watched the little group grow smaller and smaller. It was July 11, 1891.

But the wind of the open sea was in their nostrils. It felt good to have the deck of a well-built ship under their feet, a ship that obeyed the tiller's slightest move, and to hear the wind murmur "maraamu" in the rigging. No landlubbers' life could ever equal the call of adventure!

The *Papeete* was a 95-ton schooner built a few years earlier in Benicia near San Francisco. Matthew Turner's shipyard had acquired a certain celebrity in the Pacific. During this period, most of the speed records for ships sailing the Pacific were won by boats from his slipways. To build these schooners, the magnificent virgin forests of the Sierra Nevada were being exploited without restrictions; thousand-year-old giant sequoias were felled because of the remarkable constructional properties of their timber. Matthew Turner built about three hundred ships during the second half of the nineteenth century, among them three-masted barks, three-masted schooners, and brigs, but mostly two-masted schooners whose lines were familiar to anyone who knew the Pacific. He had the lion's share of all the traffic between the many archipelagos.

More than half the ships in Tahiti's local fleet—including two that belonged to the Navy—came from this shipyard. In addition to its superb construction, the California schooner was the best adapted to navigation between the islands. Weighing anywhere between 50 to 150 tons, solidly built, with relatively simple rigging, it could be handled by a very small crew—generally four men—under the command of a captain and mate. Add to that the cook and the supercargo—the officer representing the ship's owner—the total came to eight, sometimes nine men on a schooner. It also carried large whaleboats.

It should be noted that a schooner's "whaleboat" played a role almost as important as the schooner itself. Derived from boats designed for whaling, they were shorter, of broader beam, and above all, of remarkable solidity. Employing four oarsmen, they were steered by a man standing in the stern, holding an angled oar with both hands. Even today, this is the only method for embarking and disembarking on the atolls' barrier reefs or the steep basalt beaches of the Marquesas Islands where the sea roars in with such violence. Schooners often carried two whaleboats, for it was not unusual to have one break up on a reef.

The disposition of the schooner's interior was simple enough. The crew's quarters were under the forward deck, but because of the terrible heat in these tropical waters, the men were often housed in a small deckhouse between the windlass and foremast. Directly behind was the galley, then the combing around the hold. The whaleboat was lashed between the hold and the rail. Finally, the roof of the cabin stretched from behind the mainmast to the combing immediately in front of the tiller or wheel, its interior lit by portholes set in the sides, with a skylight and grating on top. Access to the cabin was by the steep companionway steps beneath the sliding hatchway and the wheel. The interior was partitioned off into one very small bunkroom for the captain and a larger one for the supercargo where he kept his strongbox, account books, and certain goods that could not be kept in the hold. It must be remembered that these schooners were first and foremost a floating commercial enterprise for buying mother-of-pearl, copra, trepang (dried sea cucumbers or sea slugs), pearls, and for selling anything that might possibly strike the fancy of the island people, from rice, preserves and flour to printed cottons, guitars and accordions. The supercargo was the most important man on board. He spoke for the commercial interests that owned the ship, he could change the itinerary at will, determine the advisability or length of a particular stay, and if, in theory, he was not supposed to interfere in navigational matters, the captain's role was not much more than an operator of a vehicle. In maritime law, this kind of navigation went by the name of "adventure," and a very appropriate name it was.

However, in cases where the captain had the owner's trust and a stake in the business, he had complete say in all transactions. That was the case with Wohler, who had long been affiliated with the Société Commerciale de l'Océanie, a German house despite its French name, with headquarters in Hamburg.

On leaving Rarotonga, the captain had announced to his crew great satisfaction that if the *maraamu* kept up, they would reach Papeete in time for July 14. He explained to the Roricks that the anniversary of the fall of the Bastille represented "the only thing the French had succeeded in instilling among the Tahitians." As he described it, "it was a bacchanalia lasting a week—sometimes more, depending on the amount of money people had to spend." Apparently they started preparing for it six months in advance, and went into debt if necessary. Tahiti was often the subject of conversation between the brothers and

Wohler as the schooner sailed close to the wind, pushed along by a steady breeze that blew even at night.

On the morning of the fifth day, the lookout pointed at a spot on the horizon and shouted "Fenua!" (Land!) It took Joseph—who was standing watch—several minutes to make out the faint motionless spot between two banks of clouds. It was Orehena, the highest point on Tahiti. Little by little, other summits began to emerge out of the bluish haze. The tip of the peninsula of Taiarapu gradually separated from the rest of the island. Toward noon, the cliffs of the *pari* became clearly visible, covered by a disheveled vegetation that hung out over the sea breaking noisily at the feet of its basalt cliffs. To the east, the coral reef marked a dividing line between the raging sea and the smooth sleek waters of the lagoon.

Gradually the mountains began to reveal their fantastic shapes, completely covered with vegetation that climbed up the most abrupt walls. Even on the topmost peaks as sharp as steeples, the silhouette of a tree stood out, as odd as it was unexpected. Waterfalls fell in successive leaps from heights lost in the clouds to the coast where they turned into torrents, then roiling brooks. This was the famous island described by Cook and Bougainville: Utopia, the land of the "noble savage," and without question, the Queen of the Southern Seas.

On the port side rose the jagged outline of Moorea, more extraordinary even than Tahiti. Whitecaps ruffled the channel between the two islands, but the *Papeete* kept up its steady course, luffing a little as it approached land. As Wohler had said, they could expect to reach their mooring by nightfall, but the *maraamu*, which had filled their sails since Rarotonga, fell all of a sudden, and the sea flattened into long and shallow undulations. They had reached the leeward side of the island. The schooner started to roll from side to side, its sails hanging limp as the men sheeted them in and hauled in on the boom tackles of the foresail and mainsail.

Occasional puffs of wind arrived suddenly, filling the sails for a moment, then seconds later, the sails dropped inert the length of the mast and rigging.

"Nothing to worry about," Wohler said to the brothers. And he assured them that they would be alongside by evening if they held to their course without drifting too much. The offshore breeze—the *hupe*—was due around eight o'clock and would get them through the channel without tacking on a sea as flat as a mirror.

The *hupe* arrived on schedule, bringing with it the fresh air of the mountains and the varied odors of land. They caught the smell of frangipani, humid earth, and ferns, mixed with whiffs of copra and vanilla. Like a stage set, the enormous mass of the mountains filled the sky, now dimly lit by the moon which had just risen on the far side of the island. A few lights blinked at the water's edge. Would that be Papeete?

The little town lay spread along the shore in the dense greenery at the feet of the oppressively high cliffs. A few outrigger canoes glided on the surface of the lagoon, the man at the bow holding a torch of blazing palm leaves in one hand, a harpoon in the other. In the darkness, the man paddling at the stern was invisible. It was like a weird ballet, with supernatural figures weaving back and forth trailing plumes of sparklers.

Dark shapes loomed on the water: cutters and schooners riding at anchor, a mailboat from New Zealand or San Francisco, a navy cutter. From the land came snatches of song and the unexpected sound of a street-organ punctuated by detonations from popguns. It was both touching and not a little unsettling to come upon a French village festival so far from home, and the din seemed out of place in this grandiose setting.

Where, Wohler and the crew wondered, were the rhythmic calls of *upa-upa,* or the curious chants of the *himene,* the ancient fugues now with biblical texts inserted by Methodist missionaries.

The rattle of the chain passing through the hawsepipe hole attracted a few bystanders on the grassy quay sparsely lit by a few gas lamps. From the whaleboat, now lowered into the water, the crew called out for someone to catch the painter so that the boat could be tied up alongside the wharf. The voices came back surprisingly clear. Once the loop of the painter had been made fast to an old cannon buried upright in the quay, the crew asked the usual question: "Eha te parau api?" (What's the news with you?)

Well, there was plenty of news. First of all, Pomare V, the last king of Tahiti, had died just a few days after their departure. He had been buried at Arue, and it had been quite a ceremony. A huge crowd had followed the funeral cortège down the missionaries' Broome Road. Most were on foot, but a few of the lucky ones rode in light California buggies pulled by small Tahitian horses. Numerous speakers had made moving speeches filled with imagery, metaphors and biblical quotations, arousing the public's wonder and admiration. And songs had been composed for the occasion—melancholy *pehe*—which brought tears to everyone's eyes. People were still talking about it a month later.

As a sign of mourning, the inhabitants of Tahiti and Moorea had abstained from their usual participation in the fourteenth of July celebrations. That was the reason for the unaccustomed tranquillity. The *Papeete*'s crew made feverish preparations to leave the ship, and there was great rejoicing when the Roricks proposed—to the captain's considerable surprise—that they stand watch on board. They said they were in no hurry; nobody was expecting them. Then Alexander added in his resonant voice: "It's been so long since we've been to a bistro that we might lose our heads." Nagel, the mate and one of the last to leave, was busying himself around the boat as the two brothers sat on the taffrail watching the crowd pressing around fair booths that proclaimed: "Spitz and his headless talking man," "Braunshwig Lottery," and "Madame Chauvin, clairvoyante."

As Nagel was about to cross the plank from the ship's stern to the quay, Alexander said half jokingly: "It would be child's play for us to set sail, wouldn't it? Just hoist the jib and foresail and gently slip anchor. Nobody would notice. The current runs toward the channel and once we're there, we'd hoist all the sails."

"Perhaps so," Nagel said, a little taken aback. "But I don't think you'd get very far. There's a navy cutter here and two armed schooners. They'd find you in no time." With that, he laughed loudly, though perhaps somewhat uneasily, and said good night.

II

IN THE PALE FRESHNESS of dawn, the brothers splashed
about in the wharf's watering place. All they could see
of the town were its commercial houses, partly hidden
behind the trunks of the poinciana lining the quay. A
fanfare of cock crows exploded on all sides. "You'd think
Papeete was a chicken coop," Alexander said with a laugh.
(Tahiti's roosters crow at irregular intervals during the
night, but respectful of tradition, they also crow at dawn.)

One after the other, white-robed shapes began to rise
from the veranda of the Société Commerciale de l'Océanie,
which was used as a dormitory by the archipelago's inhabitants when they stopped off in Papeete. Each man
carefully folded his *peue*—a mat made of woven pandanus
with a thousand uses, and his *tifaifai*, a cotton covering of
colorful patchwork. A *pareu* with its four corners knotted
served as container for the various items used in this improvised camp. The result was a clean, tidy red-and-white
bundle which the owner carried under his arm as he
moved on to the small cafés dotting the market place.

There he drank a thick, very sweet coffee served by Chinese, and exchanged the news of the day.

Seats at a table were obligingly made for the Roricks, and while their immediate neighbors feigned indifference, the rest of the room hummed with questions. "Taata itoito!" (Those sure are impressive-looking men!) was the male comment. The women nudged each other and murmured: "What handsome men! Where did these *popaa* come from?" "From Rarotonga, last night, on Wohler's schooner." "Parau mau?" (Really?) "What are they doing in Tahiti?" Elbows on the table, their chins cupped in their hands, the two strangers smiled at the commotion they were causing.

Wohler soon joined them to take them to the port authorities and police where they had to fill out the forms for entry into the territory. The Tahitian authorities were no more curious or finicky than the Rarotongans, and the brothers were permitted to stay indefinitely in "the French establishments of the South Seas." Alexander used the occasion to change the spelling of their name from Rorick to Rorique. The error had apparently been made, he said, by the German resident who drew up the official report of the shipwreck at Jaluit. They stated that they were born in South Africa of parents originally from the Isle of Jersey—which was a good explanation of their excellent French, and their impeccable English as well.

The English colony in Tahiti, being arrogant, pretentious, and of relatively long standing on the island, was delighted to entertain what it considered to be "true gentlemen." At the same time, their knowledge of German served both as introduction and recommendation to the personnel of the Société Commerciale de l'Océanie, founded in Lubeck or Hamburg, no one was quite sure which. Methodical and dogged workers, the Germans resisted anything new or unfamiliar. They lived as a clan with the sole aim of selling, every year, more and more German goods.

To the French, the Roriques were viewed as compatriots. At this time, the French population was made up of two groups: one, former military men, sailors and discharged soldiers with families, and the other, officials of the colonial administration supposedly on a five-year tour of duty. The former were good men on the whole, but noisy and unkempt, and they were always fulminating against the second group which they considered too large and much too well paid. The latter had little contact with the native population and even less with their natural environment. Avoiding the sun at all costs, they had the pallid complexion and sickly look of plants that grow in the dark.

Of Papeete's three thousand inhabitants, two-thirds were, if not pure-bred Tahitians, as least authentic Polynesians. Most of these had no ties with the place, their presence being determined solely by the existence of its natural port. As a result, fifty years earlier, the leeward side of the island had become the seat of government, the residence of Queen Pomare and her court, the center for foreign traders, missionaries of different persuasions, and a floating, mostly female, native population.

At the beginning of the nineteenth century, a few adventurous Anglo-Saxons had settled in Tahiti and married the daughters of local chiefs. Since its soil was the island's only wealth, they and their descendants had become, willy-nilly, proprietors of extensive holdings. With the creation of the port and the growth of Papeete, they began to amass large fortunes.

The wife of Pomare V was a pretty half-caste named Salmon, and she had two sisters: Mrs. Brander, married to an American, and Mrs. Atwater, the wife of a Scotsman. A few of the half-castes had been educated abroad, in Sydney and even in England, and pretended to a fairly high aristocratic level. It didn't matter whether they were descended from sailors or pure-bred Tahitians like King Pomare.

Actually no more than a large village, the town of Papeete spread out along the low, sometimes marshy, coastal plain squeezed between the shores of the lagoon and the foothills of the mountains. The houses were built of boards covered with shingles of Oregon pine, surrounded by verandas with gingerbread railings, suggesting a tropical American Far-West. In fact, some of the houses had been dismantled and transported from San Francisco. Many of them had gardens more suitable to a Paris suburb.

In the center of town, in a sort of park criss-crossed by a small brook, stood the king's palace, the governor's residence, the post office, the treasury, and buildings belonging variously to the army, navy and colonial administration. It also featured the colonials' *Cercle*, a club where the admission of a new member invariably unleashed a campaign of intrigue spiced with jealousy and malice. In front of these buildings stood a bandstand crowned with a lyre, and at the back, a "Robinson" tree house in the branches of a venerable banyan reached by a spiral staircase. Toward six in the evening, when the heat of the day had abated, bearded gentlemen sipped chilled absinthes in the aerie as they watched the high and graceful California buggies go by, some having—a considerable and conspicuous luxury—rubber-rimmed wheels.

Papeete's commercial houses stood in a row fronting the sea opposite the small island of Motu-Uta, with the jagged mountains of Moorea as a backdrop. Besides the Société Commerciale de l'Océanie, there were the New Zealand firms of Young Ltd. and Donald-Edenborough; Turner and Chapman Shipchandler, which represented the Matthew Turner Shipyards of San Francisco; Crawford and Co.; Cape Ltd. Import-Export; and finally, two with French names, Sosthène Drolet Marchandises, Générales, and Raoulx-Papineau, a Tahitian house which had recently acquired a reputation equal to that of its foreign competitors.

Several roads ran parallel to the quay, one having the unexpected name of "rue de la Petite Pologne" (Little Poland Street). Thirty years before, a native of Poland had chosen the name for a sailor's bar. Now his bar had become a respectable restaurant whose proprietor—Renvoyé, a former cook of the admiral commanding the Pacific fleet—was the uncontested master-chef of the town.

This was the curious microcosm in which the Roriques maneuvered for the next few weeks. The contrast with Penrhyn, or even Rarotonga, was staggering. There, the calm, simple, almost primitive life lacked most of the elements of civilization; here, an imitation, almost a caricature of Europe or California, but with undeniable charm. To their consternation, the use of money, not to mention its importance, which they had completely forgotten over a period of months, suddenly reasserted itself. Adding up their combined fortunes was the work of a minute: a few Australian pounds and a handful of pearls, most of them irregular, which they had received in return for teaching sail-making and carpentry in Penrhyn. Only two or three were symmetrical and of good color. Wohler suggested they offer them to Emile Levy, the local dealer in pearls, who gave them two hundred Chilean piasters, the currency then in use in Tahiti.

Thus provided, they decided to buy some respectable clothes. They had a tailor make them cotton suits of military cut with stand-up collars, whose jackets buttoned with studs. The Papeete bourgeois wore suits of blinding whiteness, starched, pressed and even waxed for greater sheen. During the course of a dinner or reception, the suit tended to develop dents and cracks at the elbows, shoulders and knees, and bulged over the chest like a medieval breastplate. For haberdashery, the brothers bought Tahitian boaters with narrow brims and high crowns, and finally, to round out their acquisitions, they rented from one Frédéric Sarciaux a tiny bungalow deep in the *purau*, on the edge of the lagoon near the temple of Paofai. They dined at Renvoyé's and in no time knew all the regulars. The Treasurer and the Attorney had tables in opposite corners; having quarreled a long time ago, their communications had ever since been confined to business matters, and these by letter only. The other functionaries grouped themselves around these two poles, thus establishing bodies of force with a neutral zone for officers of the garrison and naval station in the middle. Only whispers could be heard in the corners, while the center was often given to rambunctious behavior.

One frequent patron was a lieutenant in the naval infantry, and for some time his companion had been an oddly dressed man with a hooked nose, long hair, canvas shoes painted blue, and a multicolored bow loosely tied around his neck. Could he be an artist? "A painter!" was the excited reply. The lieutenant's name was Jenot, and his odd companion, Gauguin.

Suspicious at the beginning, the Roriques warmed to the man when they learned that he had once been a sailor. In their eyes, this was more than a recommendation; it was a title of nobility. They were amused to hear him say—as he did to anyone who would listen: "Nobody in Paris would believe me if I told them that I live in a furnished room in the house of a lady named Charbonnier, and that I dine every night between a customs officer and a receiver of registry fees. It's Europe all over again, with all its constraints, inconveniences and prejudices!"

The Roriques were in full agreement, but put off by his peculiar looks and manner, they refrained from committing themselves. After all, a sailor who had given up his calling was in their eyes a kind of renegade.

To Gauguin, who had arrived only the month before, the one thing he found to his liking was the evening rides in buggies in the company of *vahines* dressed in muslin and crowned with *tiare*, singing to the accompaniment of their accordions. Lulled by the rhythm of the sleepy little horse's trot, they would meander down the white coral road to the beach at Taunoa where they sang

[23]

and danced to the light of a kerosene lantern, sometimes until dawn.

Wohler was eager to launch his two protégés and organized a party to which he invited his friends, most of them ship chandlers and captains. Among them were Chemin, Robertson, Arnaud, André, Lucas, Martin, Garnier, the port's captain, a fellow-German named Berrüde and captain of the brig *City of Papeete*, which made the regular run to San Francisco, and Raoulx, also a former sailor and now owner of the biggest commercial house in Papeete. Being men of experience and knowledgeable about every maritime or commercial operation in the Pacific, they were greatly impressed with the Roriques. The brothers exuded energy and determination, made all the more effective by their moderation in gesture and speech.

In the company of women, on the other hand, the brothers were amiable, attentive and full of fun—in a word, irresistible. There were several young half-Tahitians with velvety eyes, a spirited young Creole whose ugly little French husband kept dogging the Roriques' heels in the hope of getting a story for his paper, the *Messager de Tahiti*, and in sharp contrast to the others, Captain André's wife, a milky blonde with periwinkle blue eyes named Lucie.

Wohler lived in Patutoa, just outside Papeete, in a spacious frame house surrounded by a large veranda on the edge of a field of sugar cane belonging to Brander. For the occasion, he had decorated the house with garlands of perfumed ferns called *maire*, and the serrated leaves of *ti* which gave off a heady odor after dark.

There is no denying that Tahiti nights are the most delicious in the world. Thanks to its temperature and peaceable atmosphere, man seems at one with nature as in no other place on earth.

During the course of the evening, Alexander found a rickety piano more or less in tune which produced some astonishing sounds, while his brother accompanied him on the flute. Then, shifting to an accordion and ocarina, they ripped off some current polkas and mazurkas that had everybody enthralled. By the end of the evening, the Roriques had won over the entire audience, naval officers as well as suspicious traders, romantically inclined young women as well as contented mothers.

For all their social success, one thing soon became clear: because of French regulations, their situation as foreigners made it impossible for them to take command of a ship, no matter how small. They could sail as mates, but since they did not wish to be separated, they agreed to a suggestion of Raoulx that they settle on the atoll of Kaukura, two hundred miles northeast of Tahiti.

At this time, the lagoon of Kaukura was one of the most fertile in pearl oysters in the Tuamotu archipelago. It was a center for pearl divers from all parts of the archipelago, as well as for representatives of the various commercial houses in Papeete who bought pearls and mother-of-pearl while selling the divers necessities along with things they could never hope to use.

As usual on such occasions, Alexander made the decision, and he opted for an immediate departure for Kaukura. Raoulx gave them a consignment of merchandise payable in pearls, mother-of-pearl and copra, without interest, for the next six months. They sailed the following week on the schooner *Mateata* which belonged to the Raoulx house and was commanded by Arnaud, a former sailor in the navy.

Kaukura, one of the atolls nearest to Tahiti, offered no passage through the reef into its lagoon. Schooners had to heave to outside the reef, with no possibility of dropping anchor because of the water's depth, then unload their passengers and cargo in whaleboats. Each trip back and forth became a small adventure. The boat had to ride in on the right wave, allowing for all the contingencies of such an operation. Depending on the condition of the sea, this could take anywhere from one to several days. As night came, the schooner had to beat out to sea and try not to go too far so as to be back by dawn of the next day. It sometimes happened that the helmsman, who had spent the day at the heavy oars of a whaleboat loaded to the gunwales, fell asleep at the tiller and woke up at dawn to find the schooner grounded on a reef.

The brothers installed themselves in the village on the edge of the lagoon, in a little house roofed with *niau*—the braided leaves of coconut palms—and stored their merchandise in a small hangar made of corrugated tin. It promised to be an austere life, but after what they had been through in Penrhyn, this was almost luxurious.

For a coral island without springs or streams, Kaukura did quite well. It had several cisterns that held enough rainwater to take care of the population, and an impressive assortment of food in its shops. During the diving season, there was a simple eating place whose proprietor—a French woman and wife of a Papeete trader—had earned a reputation for her heavy pancakes which the divers devoured with gusto. But when, after one of her hearty meals, two of the divers remained on the bottom, the pancakes were judged responsible and the lady was forced out of business.

As before, the brothers slept in their gray canvas hammocks fastened to the coconut posts supporting the house. A bayonet and two carefully oiled revolvers hung on the side wall, a curious display on this peaceful island.

The government of Tahiti had recognized the claim of the Tuamotuan inhabitants to their lagoons: only the natives had the right to fish for pearl oysters. The divers came from all the neighboring atolls—Makemo, Niau, Hikueru and Fakarava—in schooners carrying both equipment and canoes. To avoid destruction from too extensive or careless exploitation, pearl diving was permitted only periodically, island by island and in each of them, section by section. The diver and his helper made for the selected spot early in the morning, towed there with other canoes by a large cutter of shallow draught, lest it come to grief on the coral heads.

The canoes were anchored in waters that varied from 15 to 20 fathoms. When the diver was ready to descend, he lowered himself into the water up to his shoulders and held onto the outrigger of the canoe while he proceeded to inhale and exhale for a period of minutes in order to activate the oxygenation of his blood—a traditional custom handed down from father to son. The exhaling was accompanied by a long lugubrious sound, and with the last one, the diver let go, holding onto a piece of lead or iron. His companion in the canoe watched the descent through a kind of watertight spyglass. The diver's body gradually disappeared into the intense blue while the line coiled in the canoe, which was attached to the diver's lead weight, spun out with impressive speed.

In the crepuscular light of the bottom, the diver tried to find oysters in clusters and, whacking them loose with his hand protected only with a rag, detached them one by one and placed them in a weighted basket lowered from the canoe by his helper. The dive usually lasted two minutes, sometimes longer. Too long a dive exposed the man to *taravana*, the dread "bends." A good diver brought up between 150 and 175 pounds of pearl shell a day, which were sold the same evening.

Finding time heavy on their hands, the Roriques made the mistake of suggesting they take part in a dive, having already done a few in Penrhyn, but their Kaukura neighbors gave them to understand that this would spell the end of their business on the island.

In due course, the schooner *Tuamotu* stopped by Kaukura, and its captain, a man named Hoffman, told the brothers that a brand-new ship named the *Henry*, built by the Matthew Turner Shipyards for the Société Young-Maxwell, had just arrived in Papeete. André, the chief pilot, had been able to obtain a release in order to take command, but he lacked a qualified mate. Hoffman suggested that one of the brothers take the job while the other one stayed on at Kaukura. The two men exchanged glances and Joseph decided to leave the next day on Hoffman's ship.

Two days later, Joseph was on the quay at Papeete on his way to the Maxwell stores when a buggy driven by a young lady in a large Manihiki hat pulled up in front of him.

"Monsieur Rorique! I thought you were in Kaukura." It was Lucie, Captain André's wife. Gracious and smiling, with her prim little children sitting next to her, she was right out of an early nineteenth-century engraving. Joseph suddenly felt like a grubby beachcomber in his threadbare trousers, disheveled hair and eight-day growth of beard. He was also aware that he was giving stupid answers to the amiable lady's questions. Of course he remembered the party at Wohler's where he had asked her to dance. She made him promise to repeat the mazurka that had so enthralled the guests, and when he gave her an evasive reply, she threatened him with the little white leather whip she held in her hand.

"My husband will be so happy to know you are back. You are exactly the man he has been looking for." On the very next day, Joseph was hired as mate on the *Henry*, but André explained that as he himself was only a replacement for Captain Clary Wilmot while the latter was in San Francisco, André would have to give up his post when Wilmot returned.

André was as black as his wife was white. Because of his small eyes hidden under bushy eyebrows that converged over his nose, he had been given the nickname *Pua'a oviri*, meaning "wild pig." He liked to talk in a pompous manner, rocking back and forth, his hands clasped behind his back. But he was a good man, and welcomed the new arrival effusively. In point of fact, Joseph's coming greatly reduced André's work and responsibilities, for schooner captains seldom had the luck of being seconded by a European so well versed in navigation.

The *Henry*, a 110-ton ship, was a handsome specimen of California construction. Everything on board had the good smell of varnish, new timber and tar. Joseph ran his hand over the polished oak rail, tapped the stays and examined the deck rubbed smooth with holystones. "A real yacht," André said, and added that it was too bad its immaculate deck had to be stained with rancid copra oil on its very first trip.

Two days before their departure, who should turn up but Alexander. A wretched toothache had made him decide to jump aboard a passing ship in order to go to Davis, an American and the only dentist in Papeete. The sign on his office on the Quai du Commerce promised extractions "almost without pain."

Alexander came on board as the ship was being loaded, and had a long conversation with his brother in a language no one understood but assumed to be Afrikaans. Lucie's buggy often stopped on the quay next to the schooner and Joseph would leap off to talk to the young woman, a look of ecstasy on his face. Alexander was visibly displeased, and the two men exchanged sharp words—a rare occurrence for them. Alexander then returned to Kaukura and Joseph stayed with the *Henry*.

The ship's first stop was to be the island of Anaa, two hundred miles from Tahiti and one of the most beautiful of the Tuamotu atolls. The vivid emerald green of its lagoon was reflected in the clouds overhead, and it was not unusual to see a large green reflection in the sky long before the island was even visible. As with so many of the atolls, there was no passage through the reef permitting ships to anchor in the lagoon, its coral ring being virtually unbroken.

As soon as they reached the island, André disembarked to take care of certain commercial matters and only returned five days later when it was time to get under way. In his absence, Joseph was left in command and supervised the loading of mother-of-pearl and copra brought alongside by the whaleboats. Four sailors shuttled between ship and shore, each time bringing about thirty sacks which two men heaved on deck through a gangway in the bulwark. When they went back to the island, Joseph stayed at the tiller, shifting tacks constantly to be in the right spot when the whaleboat returned from shore. He found these essentially routine maneuvers exhilarating. The entire execution was up to him and him alone, he being the only man on board except for the cook, who was of little help.

To control with one hand a hundred-ton sailing ship as if it were a well-trained horse was an intoxicating experience. Two years earlier, off this very island and under the same conditions, a mate had had to take to the open sea to avoid a sudden squall. It took him two weeks to find the island again, everyone thinking meanwhile that he and the schooner were gone for good.

After Anaa, the *Henry* went to Hao to take on a load of copra. Although this large atoll has a wide and deep passage through the reef, the current rushes through it at eight to ten knots. Whenever possible, ships used the counter-current which made it possible to sail close to the shore, then, with the help of a steady breeze and a constant drift, the ship reached the opposite end of the outgoing current and entered the lagoon. But if the breeze died down or even if it weakened, the ship was at the current's mercy. Tossed about in the undertow, its tiller useless, it was carried two or three miles out to sea and the whole process had to begin again.

On certain islands, notably Takaroa, a capstan had been mounted at the narrowest point in the passage, where the current was most powerful. The crew heaved a line and hauled a hawser to the capstan and brought the ship around to where it could wait for a favorable wind to take it through. All in all, the advantages of a natural passage into a lagoon were at best relative.

The *Henry* took on two Europeans at Hao—a Protestant teacher named Louis de Verbizier and his wife—and after a stop at Fakarava, it expected to be back in Papeete on November 16. A few days later, it would leave for Apataki, whose southern extremity was barely a dozen miles from Kaukura. From one island, the other looked like a dark streak on the horizon topped by the fuzzy line of its coconut palms.

Joseph tried to persuade André to heave to before Kaukura so that he could go see his brother, who might have a shipment for Papeete, but André refused pointblank. As the ship's captain, he was determined—or so he said—to keep to a strict schedule. As a result, they were back in Papeete on December 8.

Captain Clary Wilmot returned sooner than expected, so André left the *Henry*. He recommended Joseph to his successor, but Wilmot had already hired a mate. There was nothing left for Joseph but to pack his duffle and go ashore. But not for long. That very evening, a Swedish stevedore named Axel Norman suggested he join up with the *Niuroahiti*, a small 50-ton schooner belonging to Prince Hinoi, a nephew of the recently deceased King Pomare.

Built in San Francisco and originally christened the *Dolly*, the schooner was bought by Hinoi for 3000 piasters from an American named Higgins working out of Raiatea. Hinoi rebaptized the ship, giving it the name of a native sweet-smelling flower, the *Niuroahiti*.

The transaction took place in a shop on the quay belonging to Cape next door to Raoulx's establishment. Cape was a half-Polynesian British subject born in Tahiti and was the official consignee for the *Niuroahiti*. Actually, most of the cargo belonged to him and probably part of the schooner as well. His agent and supercargo was a man named Gibson, half Tahitian and half Scot, the latter strain having taken dominion over his character.

When Joseph learned that he would be mate to a native captain, Tehahe, with only the vaguest idea of navigation who sailed more or less by instinct, he was on the point of refusing. But Gibson insisted, telling him not to worry about Tehahe. Because he, Gibson was not a French citizen, he could not take command of the ship, but in all other matters, everything would be strictly between himself and Joseph.

Until this voyage, the *Niuroahiti* had sailed only between the nearby islands: Raiatea, Bora-Bora, Moorea and Tetiaroa, an atoll owned by Hinoi about thirty miles from Tahiti. This time, they would be gone almost a month to the much more distant Tuamotus, touching at Kaukura, Fakarava, Makemo and Hao, the itinerary for the return trip to be determined by the supercargo. It was therefore necessary to have not only a skilled sailor on board but a man who could double as navigator. (For some unexplained reason—perhaps the short distances it had heretofore traveled, the *Niuroahiti* had had a frequent change of captains: Chemin in June, Matatuhe in July, Tuarii in August and finally Tehahe in September.)

In addition to the captain, mate and supercargo, the ship carried a crew of four natives: Tehanara a Terauri; Moe a Teria; Pitau a Tefaahei; and Farina a Tapaga. The first two were from the Austral Islands, the other two from Atiu, an island in the Cook archipelago. Then there was the cook, Hippolyte Mirey, a half-Tahitian born in 1865 in the district of Paea. His mother was a native of Bora-Bora, and his father a French soldier in the naval infantry discharged in Tahiti who had managed to obtain a license to run a public house. As is not uncommon, he liquidated his stock all by himself and died at thirty-nine. Hippolyte was adopted by a Tahitian couple, occasionally attended the district school, but spent most of the time playing outdoors.

By the time he was eighteen, Hippolyte, called Pori by his friends, was wandering the streets of Papeete, and committing occasional acts of larceny. Because the theft of a watch equaled six months in prison, he stole a canoe and, paddling alone, crossed to Moorea to escape the police. This sporting exploit added another six months to the six already incurred. But after serving his term in prison, he was taken on as a servant to Prince Hinoi, who had him transferred to his schooner as cook. Since the only nourishment on board consisted of preserved foods and dried beans, there was little need for a master chef.

Physically, Mirey was at a disadvantage. Many half-Tahitians are handsome, but Mirey inherited the virtues of
neither race. Of medium height, he had a weasel face with
a suggestion of Mongol, and eyes that never looked directly
at you, which gave him a shifty look.

As Joseph later described the crew: "Gibson was one of
those stolid, placid people with a very practical sense. He
was a good-tempered man whom nothing could upset. He
didn't know what fear was, just as he was incapable of
feeling. Not very talkative, he confined himself exclusively
to the care of his merchandise and to selling it at a good
price, which was perfectly commendable.

"Tehahe, the pseudo-captain, was a sort of hybrid. Vague,
soft and arrogant, like all the natives here, he had achieved
a station which, in his limited view, appeared far superior
to the others'. To his arrogance was added a half-crazed
superstitious fear. He also had seizures of ludicrous piety,
fits of violent rage and a laughable terror of water. Generally simple-minded, he would suddenly and without
warning take on the airs of a deep thinker.

"As for the sailors, they lived in the shadow of Tehahe,
their chief. None of them showed the slightest trace of
personality. They were fearful, suspicious grown-up children, and if they lacked all respect for foreigners, at least
they had some fear of their superiority. Docile above all
else, the crew executed orders without enthusiasm but also
without argument."

As soon as he came aboard, Joseph checked the inventory
of navigational instruments. He found precious little: a
compass in front of the helm, a smaller one mounted in the
cabin permitting the captain to follow the route without

leaving his bed, and an azimuth in poor condition. Joseph bought himself a spiral logbook at Cape's, and André gave him a secondhand sextant. He also purchased another revolver from Mangin, a local navy armorer who had already repaired his other two.

On the eve of departure, he was invited to dine at André's in company with Berrüde, the captain of the *City of Papeete*, and Young, the director of Young-Maxwell and the *Henry*'s outfitter.

During the course of dinner, Captain Berrüde asked Joseph:

"Did you by any chance meet an American named Charles Banks when you were in Rarotonga?"

"Yes, I did. I think he lived at Queen Makea's."

"That's him, all right!" the captain said with a cynical laugh. "So he's still living under the royal protection! Do you know that there's a reward of a thousand dollars waiting for anyone who can deliver Banks into the hands of the State of California? It's a curious story, not without some piquancy. For seventeen years, Charles Banks was a model employee of Wells, Fargo and eventually became their managing director in San Francisco. You must know it, at least by name. This was the transportation company that, up to the time the railroads reached California, connected Denver and San Francisco by way of Salt Lake City, Reno and Sacramento, using the famous pony express. Their coaches were painted bright red and pulled by four and sometimes six horses, depending on the steepness of the road, for they had to climb both the Rockies and the Sierra Nevada.

"From time to time, the convoy was attacked by Navajo

Indians but more often by desperados who infested the country when they suspected that the pony express was carrying cash. Six years ago, Wells, Fargo was robbed of a very large sum and not on the roads of the Sierra Nevada but right in San Francisco. The managing director, Charles Banks, disappeared with the cash box containing twenty thousand dollars!

"What makes the story really interesting is that Charles Banks booked passage under an assumed name on my ship, the *City of Papeete*, which was on its way back to Tahiti. This, I only learned later, of course. When he arrived in Papeete, Banks rented a house I own on the coast at Paofai. He entertained often and lavishly, then suddenly he up and left Tahiti for Rarotonga on the *Jessie Nicholls*, the same ship that brought you here from Penrhyn.

"It was just in the nick of time too. The very next day, the courier arrived from San Francisco bringing an official demand for the extradition of Charles Banks, addressed to the Governor of the French Possessions in Oceania. Now, Queen Makea had signed no extradition agreement with the British Government, so Banks was safe in Rarotonga— as long as he continued to please the queen.

"All the same, he must feel a little uneasy. Especially since Wells, Fargo, which didn't want to lose everything, has promised a quarter of the take to whoever finds it. This might well tempt some ambitious fellow, don't you think?"

"Oh, I don't know," Young said. "There may be a certain number of adventurers passing through, or even living here in Tahiti, but we don't have pirates the way they do in Micronesia.

"In 1872—I was still young then—I happened to be sail-

ing in those waters and I had an experience I'm not likely
to forget. I was working for Kapelle in Jaluit both as
captain and supercargo on the schooner *Tutuila*. The company trusted me completely. It was interested mostly in
mother-of-pearl, trepang and sandalwood, which it sold at
a handsome profit in Canton.

"So, I was plying the Carolines and Solomons, looking
for this kind of merchandise, for which I received a very
handsome commission, I must say. One day, we were sailing east of the Carolines when I noticed an odd-looking
ship in the distance. It appeared to be a schooner, but on
closer inspection, its rigging was very different. The men
on board waved to us frantically, so we sailed up to within
shouting distance.

"The ship was from Mozambique, and its owner, an aged
Arab, was on board. The captain, also an Arab, had been
heading for a port in Malay when he lost his bearings
during a storm. They had nothing to eat or drink for
several days.

"I took some provisions on board, and immediately
noted that two evil-looking Portuguese half-breeds—passengers, I assumed—had managed to terrorize the crew. The
Arab offered me his entire cargo of trepang, sandalwood
and swallows' nests for two thousand dollars. It was worth
twice that, to say the least.

"I accepted on the spot, and to transfer the cargo, we
came alongside in the lee of an atoll—actually a bank of
coral and sand a few miles away.

"But the Arab had placed a condition on the transaction: that he take his ship into a well-known port from
which he could leave as soon as some urgent repairs had

been made. I examined the map and saw that the port of Ternate was no more than a three days' sail away, so I asked Stimson, my mate, if he would agree to sail the Arab's ship. I'd give him one of my best men and take his watch on the *Tutuila*.

"Stimson said to me icily: 'If your life isn't worth more than a thousand dollars, go to it! But I have no intention of setting foot on that infidel's ship with two assassins only waiting for a chance to get their hands on the Arab's two thousand dollars.'

" 'All right, Stimson.' I said, 'in that case, I'll go alone. All I ask is that you give me your revolver. You won't need it since you're going straight back to Jaluit.'

"So I had two Colts with me, one I carried on my belt, hidden under the loose cotton tunic I always wore at sea, the second I put in the right-hand pocket of the tunic where I could pat its grip from time to time.

"I have to admit that when I saw the *Tutuila* moving away, I was suddenly seized with panic. For three days and nights, I barely slept. I didn't dare relax my vigilance for a single moment.

"On the morning of the third day, I saw land. My fears vanished and I let out a sigh of relief. That was a big mistake! Those bandits knew nothing about navigation, so that was the very moment they'd been waiting for.

"I was sitting with the Arab, next to the helm, when I heard the sound of an argument followed by screams. Suddenly, one of the Portuguese rushed toward us along the port gangway, brandishing an enormous knife. He was covered with blood, but it wasn't his. It was the captain's, whom he'd just disemboweled.

"I had my right hand on the Colt's grip in my pocket, but in a flash, I realized that I had no room to draw the revolver because I was flat up against the tiller. So I raised the Colt's barrel and shot through the pocket, which immediately caught fire.

"I hit him in the throat and he collapsed in a heap. Then I saw that the second Portuguese was poised on the deckhouse with a *krish* in his hand. By this time, I had pulled the Colt out of my pocket with my right hand, and drawn the one attached to my belt with the left. I pulled both triggers at pointblank range and hit the Portuguese in the chest, killing him instantly.

"In less than two minutes, we had three corpses lying on the deck. We dispatched the two Portuguese into the sea without ceremony. The captain we treated with some respect. Then I took counsel with the Arab.

"It was imperative that the authorities in Ternate know nothing of this drama. We made it clear to the crew that if they didn't want to spend the rest of their days in prison, they would do well to hold their tongues. We separated as soon as we arrived, and, commending my soul to Allah, the Arab paid me one hundred dollars. It's quite true that I had saved his life in saving my own.

"I had the luck to find a ship going to Manila, and once there, I picked up one of our own on its way back from Canton. I was in Jaluit a month later, everybody thinking me dead."

The audience listened to the recital with absorption and not without surprise, for it was hard to realize that this placid and respectable man who looked more like a provincial notary could be the same person who, twenty years earlier, had had such a close call under such dramatic conditions.

"Don't be alarmed, young man," Young said, turning to Joseph. "It's not likely you'll have a similar encounter on board the *Niuroahiti*. No pirate has ever ventured into the peaceful archipelago of Tuamotu."

The party broke up at a late hour, but Joseph had not been his usual lively self. He seemed pensive and distracted, and Lucie led him out to the veranda and reproached him for it.

On the morning of December 15, the *Niuroahiti* set sail after taking on two native passengers. A light breeze pushed it away from the wharf and as it sailed slowly down the coast, Lucie drove along the shore in her buggy. Joseph waved to her, and Lucie called out something but he caught only the last words . . . "when you come back."

Two days later, the *Niuroahiti* arrived at Kaukura. Alexander came on board and appeared greatly surprised to find his brother. He said he wished to go to Tahiti to pick up some merchandise. The *Niuroahiti* could drop him off at Fakarava, less than thirty miles away, where he would wait for the *Mateata* to take him to Papeete. So, the brothers were once more united on the same ship, one as mate, the other as a passenger.

Fakarava is a large atoll more than 120 miles in circumference, and its lagoon is a veritable inland sea with a wide and deep passage connecting it with the ocean. The little town of Rotoava, at the entrance, is the administrative "capital" of the archipelago. There, Alexander learned that the *Mateata* had already left, and that another ship would be very unlikely within a month. Without warning,

Joseph sudenly fell ill. Feverish and complaining of aches and pains, he took to his bed. This greatly upset Gibson.

Alexander then suggested to Gibson that since he was not eager to wait at Fakarava for a problematic ship, he would continue his trip aboard the *Niuroahiti*. Not as a member of the crew, of course, but as a replacement for his brother until he was well.

Gibson was delighted with the idea, for it meant that he could continue the trip and at no extra cost: "With two first-rate sailors on board, we'll be back in Papeete on schedule!"

When the *Niuroahiti* sailed out of Rotoava on December 28, it carried an impressive cargo: 500 piasters' worth of merchandise, twenty tons of mother-of-pearl and copra, and 3000 piasters in the supercargo's strongbox—all in all, a tempting prize for unscrupulous adventurers. At nightfall, it hove to before the atoll of Kauehi to drop a passenger. It then took a southeasterly course toward Makeno, then to Hao, its final destination.

It never reached Hao.

Days, weeks, months passed with no word of the schooner or its crew. The *Niuroahiti* disappeared between the islands of Kauehi and Makeno—less than 120 miles apart. And no storm—a distinct possibility at that time of year—was recorded.

People in Papeete began to worry, ships coming from the Tuamotus were questioned, but no one had seen the *Niuroahiti*. The ship, its cargo and the supercargo's cash box had a value of around eight thousand piasters. Its owner and shippers sent a boat to look for it. The house of Young, which also had an interest in its whereabouts, happened to have a small steamship flying the New Zealand flag, the *City of Aorangi,* in port to take on a cargo of oranges. The ship followed the *Niuroahiti*'s itinerary from Kauehi, the last port it had touched. It hugged the coast off the atolls of Katiu, Raraka and Marutea, taking the windward side of the islands in order to examine the reefs on which the schooner might have foundered. It was well known that the current between these islands could be very strong, to an extent that a ship could drift miles in a single night. But the *City of Aorangi* returned to Papeete two weeks later having seen nothing and learned nothing of the fate of the *Niuroahiti.*

III

ON THE 3D OF MARCH, 1892, a schooner sailed through the north passage leading into the lagoon of Ponape, an island in the Carolines which, at that time, was under Spanish rule. In the blinding light of noon and the glint of the lapping waves, two small coral islands emerged on either side of the passage. The schooner hugged the wind to avoid a reef to the west, then ran free on a port tack.

The Rarotongan flag hung from its mainsail and its transom carried the inscription *Poe,* and under that, *Avarua.* What was this schooner doing so far from its home port of Rarotonga?

But the most amazing thing was the way the *Poe* resembled the *Niuroahiti,* last seen in the Tuamotu archipelago: the same streamlined shape, the same peculiar deckhouse, the same navy blue hull.

All doubts vanished when Joseph Rorique's silhouette appeared at the helm, and on the port side near the davit, Alexander's in conversation with a native pilot. Then who should emerge but Mirey, his anxious, servile face framed in the galley doorway. The crew, who looked like Tahitians except for being shorter and darker-skinned, were manning the ship—and very well too—in response to Alexander's imperious commands in *beach la mar*, the lingua franca of the Pacific.

What had happened to the crew taken on in Tahiti? Where were Captain Tehane and Gibson, the supercargo? Why had the name, home port and flag been changed?

After a three-mile sail across the island-studded lagoon, the *Poe* took a southeasterly course toward the island of Langar. With its sails gradually lowered, the ship coasted under its own momentum toward the opening of the narrow channel that led to Colonia de Santiago—plain Colonia to the Spaniards—where it dropped anchor. The *Poe's* neighbor on the left was a small cruiser, the *Don Juan de Austria*, and on the right, what appeared to be an unarmed warship, the *Dona Maria de Molina*.

Seen from a distance, Ponape's volcanic formation and dense vegetation were reminiscent of the Samoan and Society Islands. Closer, the difference was dramatic. Between the coastal plain and the lagoon stretched a virtually impenetrable mangrove swamp. There were coconut palms and the areca palms which produce the betel nut chewed throughout Malay, and sago palms, the marrow of a single stalk providing a family food enough for a week. There were also species of animals unknown in Polynesia, including bats, batrachians, saurians and even snakes. The proximity to the Celibes and New Guinea was already noticeable. As for Colonia itself, it seemed no different from all the other Pacific villages built on stilts.

As soon as the *Poe* had moored, a naval vessel came churning through the water to inspect it. An officer and

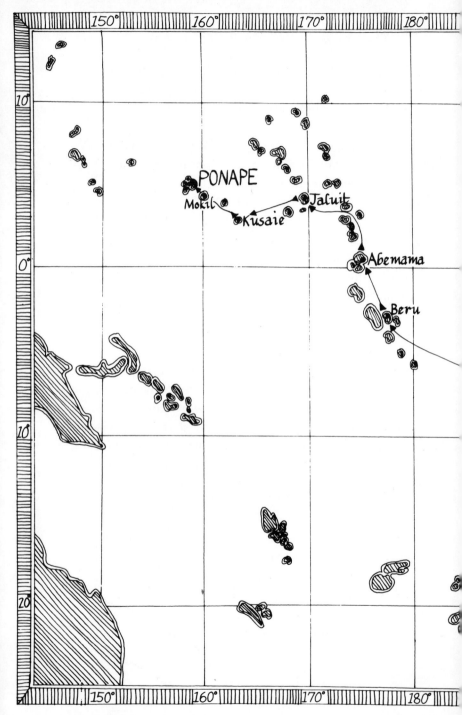

PONAPE

Mokil

Kusaie

Jaluit

Abemama

Beru

The South Sea Voye

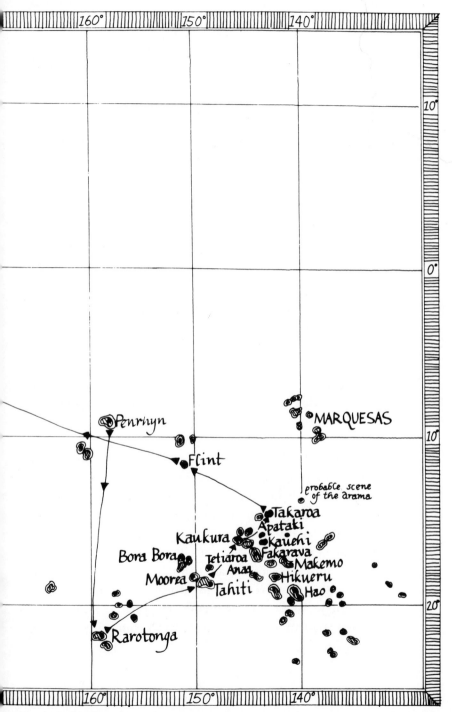

the Rorique Brothers

doctor came aboard and asked to see the ship's papers: the list of its crew members, health certificate and ship's manifest. The list of crew members, drawn up in Rarotonga, carried the stamp "Collector of Customs, Port of Avarua" and mentioned only three men: Georges de Vernier, captain; Louis Toussaint, his associate; and Polydor Dessart, cook, a native of the Antilles, borne out by his swarthy complexion. Its sailors had been recruited on the island of Peru during the course of a stop in the Gilberts. Apparently, Georges de Vernier had acquired the schooner—and a very good bargain too, he was pleased to say—at Rarotonga with the intention of trading among the various archipelagos, but mainly the Carolines, which were in a free zone that dispensed with customs. In point of fact, he happened to have a very interesting cargo on board and was anxious to dispose of it as quickly as possible. Because the Rarotongans were such landlubbers, he had not been able to recruit a crew there, so he had been forced to sail with only three aboard, a risky venture but less so than waiting forever at their precarious mooring at Avarua during the height of the cyclone season.

The officer took the papers with him to show to the military governor. A series of local disturbances had placed the island in a state of siege. For some years now, the Spaniards had been running into difficulties in the archipelago—where their authority was at best minimal—because of the influx of Britons, Germans and Americans. In fact, the Americans had maintained successful Baptist, Seventh-Day Adventist and Mormon missions for half a century. When the Spaniards regained the archipelago, they tried to expel the missionaries, but without success.

Bitter religious strife had been added to the struggle for power, with each denomination taking arms against the other. There had been several wounded and even a few dead.

During the afternoon, Alexander set off in the whaleboat with three native sailors. He wished to reclaim his ship's papers from the "Commandacia" and give them the details of the ship's itinerary.

With his tall spare figure, smart white cotton suit with stand-up collar and wide-brimmed Manihiki on his head, Captain Georges de Vernier made a striking impression on the Commandante. The *Poe*'s papers were duly signed and stamped, and returned to him with great courtesy. Whistling with satisfaction, the captain sauntered back to the wharf where he had an appointment with a German merchant from Ponape named Narrhum. The German had already agreed to help him sell his cargo and was to come aboard for the purpose the following day. Narrhum now invited him to have a drink at the bar-restaurant he owned, where he introduced Alexander to his *vahine*, a pleasant Polynesian woman of about thirty who happened to be a native of Rarotonga. What luck to go aboard a ship from her own country! She had left Rarotonga at fifteen, having been abducted by a Norwegian captain named Larsen who abandoned her in Tahiti, which she subsequently left with a Greek. Captain de Vernier, wishing to change the subject, asked Narrhum to furnish the *Poe* with fresh food and water.

The whaleboat returned to the ship with the provisions and also with three ladies whom the gallant captain had invited aboard. To the unprepared cook, Alexander announced: "Pori, all is well: our papers are in order. And look what I've brought you! We're going to have a real *maa*—a far cry from our usual fare." Mirey outdid himself; the company sang his praises and that of his wines. And since the captain and his mate were gifted musicians, things were lively on board the *Poe* that night.

The next morning, the deck of the schooner was thronged with visitors. Narrhum came with his wife, together with other buyers and a number of curiosity seekers, for a ship from Rarotonga was a very unusual event in Ponape.

Staring hard at the captain and his mate, Narrhum exclaimed: "It's amazing how you remind me of two sailors I saw in Jaluit three years ago. They were also brothers and had come from San Francisco on a cutter. I didn't know them well, but I remember they had exactly your build."

The schooner's large cabin had been turned into a store where Mirey—alias Polydor Dessart—measured out and sold printed cottons. It was unfortunate that he spoke only French, a language unknown on the island. But suddenly, unexpected help turned up in the person of Narrhum's *vahine* and her companion, the Tahitian wife of another German. She and Mirey started talking in the languid sing-song French with the rolling "r's" peculiar to Polynesia. She suddenly sensed that she was conversing with a countryman who didn't wish it to be known. "Ite oe parau Tahiti?" (Don't you speak Tahitian?) Mirey was taken aback and, looking nervously toward Joseph at the other end of the cabin, said "Oia" (That's right) under his breath. The man looked so dismayed that after exchanging knowing glances, the two ladies decided to say no more.

Meanwhile, Narrhum and the captain had gone down to the hold to see what the German might find of interest. After tasting a sample of New Zealand corned beef, Narrhum bought two cases. "I see you've also been to Tahiti," he said. "No, we haven't," the captain replied. Narrhum pointed to some cases clearly marked "Donald, Papeete." "Oh, those . . . Perhaps you aren't aware that Donald-Edenborough has two branches, one in Rarotonga and one in Papeete. The *Richmond*, which does the Auckland run, stops first at Rarotonga and sometimes the cargo destined for Tahiti is taken off by the Rarotonga branch." "I see," Narrhum said. But as he was climbing back to the deck, his eye fell on sacks of sugar and flour heaped in a corner of the hold labeled "Young—Papeete" and "Raoulx—Papeete."

The transaction proved very successful, and the *Poe*'s cargo diminished as if by magic. Even a few Spanish officers came on board, but Captain de Vernier seemed nervous and eager to set sail as soon as possible. Narrhum's wife asked him to postpone his departure so that he could take on two American deserters who lived on the southern end of the island, but he refused flatly. "But," Narrhum protested, "you told me you wanted to get rid of your sailors from the Gilberts. You said they were worse than useless . . ." "That may be," the captain replied, "but it doesn't follow that I want to take on two complete strangers, and deserters at that. That could be very risky; I have no desire to be thrown to the sharks."

The two men made arrangements to meet at Narrhum's

the following day, a Sunday. The *Poe* would set sail on Monday. That evening, not three but five ladies spent the night on board, and made so much noise, so late, that the commander of the *Don Juan de Austria*, anchored a hundred yards off, ordered his spotlight lit and trained on the offending schooner.

The next morning, Mirey had to wait until ten o'clock before he could serve coffee. The captain, his mate and the guests lay scattered about the cabin. In a thick voice, the captain informed the cook that he could go ashore for the day, for which Mirey thanked him profusely. Leaving two sailors on board, the entire company eventually met at Narrhum's. Throughout the afternoon, Captain de Vernier and Louis Toussaint drank heavily, and at six o'clock, Mirey warned them that it would now be too late to prepare a meal on board. So they all repaired to a restaurant, and although the captain and his mate were steady enough, both were obviously quite drunk. Finally, overcome by their excessive intake of spirits, the brothers left the party. Mirey, who had drunk nothing, appeared to be deeply troubled. Taking advantage of the brothers' absence, he retired to a corner of the room with the Tahitian lady and Narrhum's wife and talked to them with feverish intensity.

"Please take me to a magistrate," he pleaded to the ladies. "I have to tell somebody what happened on that ship. It was terrible! Yes, I am from Tahiti. The others came aboard in Tahiti too. But they are all dead now—murdered by those two brothers . . ."

Just then, Captain de Vernier, who a moment ago would have seemed incapable of such an exploit, leapt through a window of the veranda shouting: "Pori, it's time to go!" And he added: "Don't pay any attention to him. He always tells the same wild stories when he's drunk." When the cook refused to move, Alexander grabbed him by the shoulders. Narrhum, who had been listening, broke in: "Take your hands off that man!" "Mind your own business!" the captain bellowed. As he started to shove Mirey through the door, he made the mistake of jostling Narrhum. The German let go with a hard jab at his abdomen which sent the captain reeling to the floor—not too difficult a feat in view of his general condition. Narrhum was on his way to the door when he saw Louis Toussaint coming at a run. As the mate rushed up the veranda steps, Narrhum, who was standing at the top, gave him a sharp kick in the temples. The effect was immediate: Toussaint rolled down the stairs and collapsed among the hibiscus surrounding the veranda.

Although the drama lasted only a moment, it caught the attention of a guard on patrol. To his inquiries, Narrhum replied: "It's a good thing you've come. Keep everyone here while I go report to the officer on duty." He disappeared into the night and after a protracted search, returned to the restaurant with the officer. What was his surprise to find Mirey flanked by two soldiers. The captain and his mate had succeeded in persuading the guard to arrest Polydor Dessart—it appeared that he was a little weak in the head—and take him back to the ship. The officer ordered the cook released so that he could interrogate him. Captain de Vernier and Louis Toussaint were free to return to the *Poe*. For the moment, it was judged to be nothing more than a drunken quarrel and a general disturbance of the peace. But Narrhum insisted that an interpreter take down Mirey's deposition. This proved difficult in view of the lateness of the hour, but in the end, they finally found an officer who spoke French and another who spoke English. The cook was reasonably fluent in both: moreover, he appeared to be perfectly sane and not at all under the influence of alcohol.

The cook's deposition was taken in a room in the guardhouse lighted by a single lantern hanging from the wall. It lasted two hours. Though intimidated at first by the three Spanish officers seated opposite him at a long table, his voice gradually grew firm as, shifting between jolting English and hesitant French, he recited the following story:

"My name is not Polydor Dessart but Hippolyte Mirey. I am not from Martinique but from Tahiti. Those two men are brothers—Alexander and Joseph Rorique. The schooner *Poe* is actually the *Niuroahiti*, owned by Prince Hinoi Pomare, on which we set sail from Papeete on December fifteenth of last year. I haven't been able to say anything until now because they forbade me on pain of death to speak any language but French.

"On the night of January fifth, we were in the vicinity of the island of Makemo in the Tuamotus. I was asleep in the cabin, as was Gibson, the supercargo, and Joseph Rorique, who said he was sick. Because of the heat, Tehahe, the captain, had gone to sleep on the roof alongside the deck skylight. About ten o'clock, we were suddenly woken up by the sound of shooting. We recognized the sound because the two brothers liked to pass the time shooting at sea birds. Gibson jumped out of his bunk and asked me in Tahitian: 'What are those *popaa* shooting at at this time of night?' He climbed up to the deck, I followed, and noticed in passing that Joseph's bunk was empty. Gibson had barely reached the companionway when Alexander rushed up to him, waving his revolver: 'Well, well,' he said, 'this is just what I've been waiting for!' He shot him pointblank. Gibson reeled and fell face down on the port deck. By the light of the binnacle lamp, I could just make out Tehahe's body lying near him, and Joseph standing by the helm, a revolver in his hand. I wondered if I was dreaming or had suddenly gone mad. I was standing half out of the companionway when Alexander aimed at me and shouted: 'Go back down or I shoot!' I heard two more shots—probably to finish Gibson off—then Alexander's voice saying to Joseph: 'Lash the tiller and come give me a hand.'

"From the porthole in the deckhouse, I watched the brothers pick Tehahe up by the arms and feet and heave him overboard. Gibson gave them more trouble because he was heavier. Then they slushed the deck with several bucketfuls of water and swabbed it vigorously. There was blood everywhere. Then they ordered me to come up. I was sure they were going to kill me, so I fell on my knees and begged them to spare me. 'We'll see about that later. Meanwhile, go tell Teria to take the watch and warn the others to stay below. If one of them comes up on deck, he's a dead man. Now go make us some coffee.'

"He followed me into the galley. By the light of the hurricane lamp, I could see that his shirt—it was a regular striped sailor's shirt—was covered with blood. Probably Gibson's, when he lifted him under the armpits. He noticed it too, peeled it off, rolled it into a ball, and threw it into the sea. As he was leaving, he took the knives and cleaver I had lined up on the kitchen table. Then he ordered me into the cabin. At six in the morning, I was called up on deck, all the men were summoned, and Alexander announced that from now on he was captain. And he added that no one would be hurt if they obeyed, their wages would be paid, and those who wished to leave the ship would be given ample provisions and dropped off on Morura, an uninhabited island where they could be picked up by a passing ship. They asked me if I wanted to leave, but I was afraid of a trap and said I'd already run into trouble with the law in Tahiti and wasn't eager to be interrogated again and maybe put in prison. I'd rather stay on the ship with them. That seemed to satisfy them.

"While all this was going on, everybody had forgotten about the passenger, a native named Fateria. We hadn't seen him since we left because he'd fallen sick and kept to his bed. One of the crew came to tell Alexander that the passenger was worse and Alexander gave the sailor a cup with some liquid in it which he said would make him feel better. By noon, the man was dead. The body was brought on deck. They wrapped it in two copra sacks sewn together, Alexander draped a French flag over it and asked one of the sailors to say a few prayers before they pitched it into the sea.

"I thought this was strange, seeing that the night before, Tehahe and Gibson had been thrown overboard without ceremony. I also realized that the ship was now heading in a northwesterly direction, which meant we weren't going to Tahiti. One of the sailors told me he thought we might be heading for the island of Flint.

"The Roriques spent the whole day looking for the *Niuroahiti's* papers. They asked me if I knew where they were, but of course I didn't. They finally found them in a zinc box on top of Tehahe's locker. They inspected them, then wrapped them up in a bundle, weighted it with a piece of metal and threw it into the sea. Then they sat down at the hatchway table and went to work with brushes and stamps. The papers they made up that day are the ones they presented here when we arrived. They also cut up a French flag and, using the red and white parts, made the Rarotonga flag that's now flying on the ship.

"Then they let down the whaleboat and rowed it to the stern, where they removed the lead letters off the transom. Using the ones that made up *Niuroahiti Papeete,* they put together *Poe Avarua.* It took a lot of work, for they were missing an 'A' and a 'V,' so some of the letters had to be reshaped. They also had a lot of trouble putting them back on. After that, they painted over the old names on the two life preservers astern and replaced them with the new.

"On January eleventh, Alexander gave me a bottle of rum and told me to give it to the crew. Two of the men drank some, but the other two refused because they had promised their priest not to drink any spirits. I brought the bottle back to Alexander, and he told me to give the men some tobacco.

"Toward evening, everybody was called up on deck to reef the mainsail. Two of the sailors—those who had drunk the rum—were sick. They collapsed on the deck and started vomiting. Their faces had gone livid and they were moaning with pain. Everybody was alarmed. Alexander insisted they had contracted Fateria's disease, that they were about to die and we should get rid of their bodies as fast as possible. Alexander ordered them thrown into the sea although we could see that one of them was still alive.

"After this, the two surviving sailors refused to eat what I cooked. They lived off bananas and coconuts we'd taken on in Fakarava and spent their days below when they weren't on duty.

"On the morning of January seventeenth, Alexander gave the sailors orders to lower the flying jib. They ducked under the bowsprit and past the bobstay, which wasn't easy, for the sea was very rough. They were drenched. Just then, Alexander asked me to go find him a bottle of beer in the cabin. Looking through the porthole, I could see Alexander on the davit with a revolver in his hand. He was shouting to the men: 'Faster, or I shoot!'

"The schooner was sailing on the port tack, and all of a sudden, there were the two sailors' heads bobbing in the water on the starboard side. They must have jumped into the sea to escape Alexander. Joseph, who was at the helm, didn't turn a hair, and the ship kept right on its course. I came up with the bottle of beer. 'Pori,' Alexander said, 'go see what those men are doing in the bow.' I came back and told him: 'There's nobody there.' 'Those stupid fools! They must have thrown themselves into the sea. That's the end of them; we're at least fifty miles from Penrhyn.' That's how I learned where we were.

"With that, the Roriques began to enjoy being masters of the ship. They hoisted an American flag and saluted it with revolver shots and sang 'Jolly Roger.' They told me to join in the celebration, but I was too scared to make a sound.

"A few days later, we came to the islands of Byron and Sydney, but when the brothers saw the British flag flying, they decided to go on to Peru, where a native pilot sailed the boat up to its mooring. A white trader and a missionary came aboard. Alexander told them that his crew had deserted, so the trader found him three natives from the island who agreed to come aboard as crew. We set sail the next day for Apamama, an atoll with a large lagoon and a good deep passage which the Roriques seemed to know well. An American schooner, the *Equator*, was also moored there. The brothers already seemed to know the captain, a man named Cameron. They bought a Winchester rifle, some beer and a case of gin from him, and paid for it with flour and sugar. Tembinoka, the king of Apamama, came aboard too and bought some things he paid for with copra. There was a rumor going around that the Roriques had been there three years before and had left without paying the king the tax due on their merchandise. Our new sailors warned us to be on the alert because Tembinoka might order the ship seized. His men could well cut away the sails and remove the rudder to keep us from leaving. So we set sail during the night of February twenty-third.

"We had just gotten under way when we hit some very bad weather. One of the sailors made a stupid maneuver, letting go the foresail, which put us athwart a wave. My saucepans flew in all directions, the china broke, the stove was torn from its moorings. The guilty sailor was tied to the mast and Joseph thrashed him with a rope. We reached Kusaie the next day but had to wait several days for the right winds to blow us through the passage.

"There was an American missionary and his family in Kusaie. Some passengers for Pingelat came aboard, among them a woman who appeared to be Spanish. The Roriques installed her in the cabin as far as Mokil, where she got off without having to pay her passage. From Mokil, we finally headed for Ponape. I decided to desert there; I knew they were only waiting for the right moment to get rid of me."

It was almost midnight by the time Mirey finished his deposition.

"Arrest me, put me in prison if you think I deserve it, but on no account will I go back on that ship!"

The officers were impressed with Mirey's sincerity and discussed what they should do next. The facts the cook had furnished them would be easy enough to verify, but they would have to get permission to make the investigation and, if need be, search the *Poe*, which might already be far out to sea.

Don José Padrinan, the military commander who also functioned as governor, had told them that evening that he felt tired and unwell and didn't wish to be disturbed. All the same, one of the officers decided to wake him and tell him what was going on. His disobedience was received with ill humor, but the governor gradually calmed down and gave him written orders to give to the commander of the *Don Juan de Austria*. They must do everything to make sure the *Poe* did not set sail, and get their hands on its captain and mate.

The night was very dark and still, making it unlikely that the schooner would sail, at least before dawn. Commanded by an ensign, about fifteen marines from the *Don Juan de Austria* silently boarded a whaleboat and a large canoe. Mirey had warned them: "You'd better be on your guard, for they are well armed and very good shots." The two boats moved noiselessly toward the dark shadow floating on the water. A faint light from the east revealed that the *Poe* was still at its mooring, but it appeared to be deserted. The canoe came alongside, four men pulled themselves up, leapt over the bulwark and flattened themselves against the wall of the galley. The captain and his mate must have been expecting this visit, for they suddenly erupted, Alexander with a rifle, and Joseph a revolver in each hand. "Brazos arriba!" (Hands up), they shouted. Five guns from the whaleboat in the shadow of the *Poe* pointed at them. The answer came back: "Drop those guns!" Furious, the brothers let them fall to the deck and gave themselves up. The men climbed aboard, seized the brothers and put them in handcuffs. A few minutes later, they were in the boats. Captain de Vernier's assurance suddenly returned: "What is the meaning of this unpleasantness, sir?" he asked the ensign. "May I see your orders?" "You'll see them soon enough, when I take you before the commander."

The first interrogation took place on board the *Dona Maria de Molina*.

"You are accused of assassinating the captain, super-

cargo and crew of the schooner in order to take possession of it. You falsified its name and home port. In addition, your identities are false. Your names are Alexander
and Joseph Rorique."

The *Poe*'s captain protested loudly, maintaining that
the whole story was invented by that fool of a cook, Mirey.

"If you were as innocent as you claim, why did you try
to defend yourselves and shoot our marines?"

"Because this country is in a state of siege," Alexander
snapped back. "We were afraid of an attack by desperados
disguised as marines. As you know, that happened recently in the Philippines."

The captain and his mate then claimed they had no
idea who the Roriques were. They swore under oath—for
they had not been indicted yet—that they were Georges
de Vernier, a captain in the merchant marine, aged thirty-
five and born on the Isle of Jersey, and Louis Toussaint,
pilot, age twenty-seven, born in Saint-Polm, New Bruns-
wick, Canada.

One thing struck everyone: the many physical traits
they had in common, and the similarity in their voices.
Narrhum, who had been summoned, stated: "When I saw
them together, I recalled having seen them in Jaluit three
years ago. It was said that they were two brothers who had
come from San Francisco on a cutter which they tried to
sell, but its papers weren't in order."

The public prosecutor for the Carolines immediately
appointed an investigating commission. It included Luis
Roldan y Torci, the purser on the *Dona Maria de Molina*,
and two officers, Jocinto Vidal and Enrique Vidauretta.
By afternoon, the commission was on board the *Poe* and

examining it in detail. Before they had gone aboard, they had looked at the transom which read *Poe Avarua*, but it was obvious that the letters were of recent vintage; besides, as Mirey had said, the letters "V" and "A" were crudely made because of the limited tools they had on board. Also, the imprint of the original letters spelling *Niuroahiti Papeete* was still visible.

An inventory of the cabin revealed still more evidence: First, hanging under the companionway steps, they found three oilskins of American make, each with a strap for closing the collar in case of heavy rains. Each strap had a small triangle of cloth on which was written the name of its owner: One read W. Gibson, another Tehahe, a third, J. Rorique. These were precisely the people Captain de Vernier pretended not to know.

Several letters turned up in a drawer, as well as rubber stamps, one of them spelling out "Collector of Customs, Port of Avarua," identical to the one on the list of crew members they had presented on their arrival in Ponape. The commission also discovered an official German stamp, more exactly a bronze seal, the very one stolen from the Marshall island resident in Jaluit. Narrhum told the Spaniards that in 1889, the German resident had reported the disappearance of his seal while it was temporarily being used on the gunboat *Wolf*. In the captain's closet, they found two notebooks: on one was written "Rorique Brothers," and on the other, "Alexander and Joseph Rorique." The first was a ship's log, the second a collection of observations and nautical calculations. A reading of the first corroborated certain events already mentioned by Mirey, such as the taking on of the three sailors in

Peru, the meeting up with the schooner *Equator*, and the incident with the king of Apamama, as well as the passage from Kusaie to Mokil "worked" by the handsome Creole.

There was no point looking for a description of what transpired on the night of January 5 or any of the other events related by Mirey, for the journal only began with the date January 18, and the heading on its first page read "Continued." All attempts to find the preceding notebook proved fruitless. Finally, as a last proof and not one of the least, the commission noticed that the deck on the portside next to the deckhouse was deeply gouged in two places. The armorer on the commission had little trouble identifying these gouges as the tracks of bullets shot at pointblank range. The first hole would probably produce nothing, since the bullet had surely been removed already, but the second brought forth a bullet under a layer of oakum. When the armorer finally extricated it, it turned out to be of the same caliber and make as those in the revolver found on board.

Thus, the results of the investigation did indeed confirm the cook's shocking tale. On the strength of these, the public prosecutor decided to indict Captain Georges de Vernier and his mate, Louis Toussaint, on grounds of piracy and murder. Mirey and the three sailors from the Gilberts would be held at the disposition of the court. As the schooner had originally sailed under French colors, those indicted would be taken by the next mailboat to Manila, the administrative capital of the region, where a French consul was in residence. In the meantime, they would be kept separated and in irons on board the *Don Juan de Austria*.

There they stayed almost a month until the *Venus* put in at Ponape. Handcuffed, their feet attached to an enormous iron bar, they were placed in steerage on a curved and therefore very uncomfortable hatch cover. The two brothers protested to Aguilar, the junior officer who had originally arrested them on the *Poe* and was now charged with accompanying them to Manila. Aguilar replied dryly that for a pair of assassins, they were already being treated far too well. Alexander spat at him, the officer blanched at the insult, charged on Alexander and kicked him in the groin. At that, Joseph reared up, grabbed the officer's left leg and bit him in the calf with all the strength of his incisors. It took three men to free Aguilar.

After a hard beating, the brothers' wrists were tied behind their backs, but even so, everyone kept his distance as if they were a pair of wild beasts.

It so happened that when they stopped at Guam, an American trader came on board the *Venus*, and such was his hatred of the Spaniards that he expressed some sympathy for the brothers. This did nothing to alleviate their treatment. They arrived in Manila on May 10, 1892, and since the monsoons had not yet begun, the city was stifling. Flashes of lightning streaked the gray sky but not a drop of rain fell.

Their arrival, however, was a kind of deliverance. Their feet were freed from the iron bar and they had only to wear handcuffs. They were taken to the prison of Billibid on the road between Manila and Quezon, where they were left in a large room with other detainees. Mirey and the three unfortunate sailors from Peru—Baku, Karotu and Nako, who understood nothing of what was going on —were put in the Casa Privilegia, where they had a little freedom, limited of course to the confines of the prison walls.

IV

UNLIKELY AS THESE INCIDENTS may seem today, they were far from rare in the Pacific of the nineteenth century and even at the beginning of the twentieth. How many disappearances attributed to navigational accidents were in fact due to acts of piracy will never be known. Obviously, the only ones we know about are those where the pirates were caught. At about the same time, two other acts were committed bearing certain similarities to the case of the *Niuroahiti.*

On January 20, 1893—or it could have been a year later—the *Hesper,* a three-masted bark flying American colors, also happened to find itself in the vicinity of Penrhyn. It was making a trip from Newcastle in Australia to San Francisco with a load of coal. The captain was a big blond Viking by the name of Sodergeen who had just been married and, following the Nordic custom, had his bride on board. The first mate was named Lucas and the second mate, Fitzgerald. Among the crew was a man named Saint-Clair, a bully who fancied himself a would-be pirate. He claimed that the *Hesper* was carrying twenty thousand dollars in gold. All the crew needed to do was follow his orders, get rid of the captain and his officers, and the ship would be theirs. They would then sell the ship in a port where the authorities were not too particular about formalities. Two of the sailors, Sparff and Hansen, took to the idea, and so the three men launched a campaign to reduce the rest of the crew to silence.

That particular night, the second mate was on duty from 8 o'clock to midnight. Toward eleven, he was called to the bow by one of the men at the cathead, under the pretext that one of the sails was damaged. Suspecting nothing, Fitzgerald went up, was promptly knocked senseless and thrown into the sea. A little before midnight, Lucas, the first mate, was about to take the watch when he was called from a porthole. But instead of finding Fitzgerald there, as was usually the case, it was one of the sailors. Justifiably suspicious, he went to the captain to express his concern. The captain laughed and tried to reassure him: "Come, let's go see for ourselves," he said. But his wife was frightened and implored him to take his revolver. "If it makes you happier," he said and walked down the passageway that led to the deck door. Lucas flung the door open and flattened himself against the wall. He just had time to see Saint-Clair and Sparff, each armed with a handspike and in an attitude that left no doubts as to their intentions. The captain fired, as did Lucas, but their assailants disappeared. The captain shouted for everyone to come on deck. The crew appeared, as did the three men on watch—Saint-Clair, Hansen and Sparff. Sodergeen immediately put them in irons until he could decide what to do with them.

A century earlier, a captain in the same situation would have lost no time passing sentence and even seeing to its execution. In 1893, the guilty had to be turned over to the judiciary in the nearest country. After a glance at the map, the captain concluded it was Tahiti.

So, five days later, the *Hesper* sailed into the port of Papeete. Artaud, the public prosecutor for the French Republic, realized to his considerable displeasure that he had to take the three men into custody and embark on proceedings with the American judiciary in San Francisco, that being the *Hesper*'s home port. This would take time, for captains of ships plying between Tahiti and California were not eager to take on such passengers. In the end, the captain of the *Galilee*, a man named Paulsen, was requisitioned to take them on and agreed on condition that the three would be kept separated and in chains in the bottom of the hold, and that three armed men, one a French gendarme and two *mutoi*—Tahitian policemen—would accompany them.

Saint-Clair was sentenced to death on May 23, 1893, but owing to the interminable delays already customary in American justice, he was not hanged—at St. Quentin—until May 1895. Sparff and Hansen were sentenced to hard labor for life and finished their days in a penitentiary.

The actors in the second drama arrived quite by chance and by a curious coincidence, on this same island of Apamama in the Gilberts, sixteen years after the Roriques.

On the morning of January 24, 1908, the crew of an Australian schooner, the *Louise Kenny*, moored in the lagoon, noticed that a 100-ton schooner had come to grief on the reef. The crew hurried to the ship to try to save it.

The schooner, the *White Rose* from Valparaiso, had lost its keel and rudder, its hull had been staved in by the reef and was full of water. Near the shipwreck they found two men, John Taylor from Manchester, a powerfully built man of about thirty with a thick black beard who claimed to be the owner, and George Jackson from London, a thin blond boy not over twenty; the two men constituted the entire crew. Taylor told the sailors from the *Louise Kenny* that they had been wrecked just before dawn, having sighted the reef too late to avoid it. Nor did they have the faintest idea where they were. They had left Valparaiso for Tahiti, but had decided to change course and head for Sydney. A couple of ancient maps and a malfunctioning sextant apparently were their only navigational instruments.

Taylor suggested to Bradshaw, the captain of the *Louise Kenny*, that he buy the *White Rose*, but Bradshaw refused. Taylor then offered to sell him the anchor, chain and mast, but again without success.

Taylor and Jackson were taken in hand by the local magistrate who served as representative of the British administration on Tarawa. In 1908, the heroic days of Tembinko and the exploits of that curious potentate of the Southern Seas who had so enthralled Robert Louis Stevenson were only a dim memory.

Two days later, the *Louise Kenny* set sail for Tarawa with the two shipwrecked passengers on board. Captain Bradshaw, having carefully inspected their ship, placed little faith in the two men's story, or more exactly Taylor's, for Jackson had not mentioned any of these events. Jackson even seemed anxious to tell him something, but he was clearly terrified of his companion, who never allowed him out of his sight. However, taking advantage of a moment's inattention on Taylor's part, Jackson managed to convey to the *Louise Kenny*'s supercargo some very revealing facts concerning the *White Rose*, one being that its real name was the *Nueva Tigre*. When informed of this, Bradshaw—whose suspicions were already well aroused —decided on a course of action. The *Louise Kenny*, with its cargo and strongbox containing several hundred pounds sterling, was a compelling temptation for a determined pirate, and Bradshaw had no intention of waiting until they reached Tarawa.

There were only three Europeans on board: the captain, the supercargo and the cabin boy. In case of attack, they could hardly depend on the native sailors. So he must act quickly. Taylor was knocked out with a bludgeon and unconscious just long enough to be put in irons and shut up in the forward berth. There he stayed, covered by Bradshaw's revolver, until their arrival in Tarawa. When the two men were turned over to the British authorities, Jackson's deposition divulged the astonishing adventures of the *White Rose*.

Jackson's real name was Frederick Skerrit and he was indeed from London. Taylor's name was actually Mortelman and he was Belgian. The two men had come to know each other while sailing from Scotland to Callao on the cruiser *Almirante Grau*, built at Barrow-on-Furness for the Peruvian Navy. They disembarked in Callao in 1907, and spent their time going from bar to bar until, for lack of money, they were forced to join up as sailors on the *Nueva Tigre*. A pretty 100-ton schooner built in

1902, it had been bought for $6500 by an Italian, Juan Cafiero, in Valparaiso who registered it in Peru. (An interesting detail: the wheel of the helm had belonged to another ship and bore the name *Puelche*.) Juan Cafiero died in 1903, leaving a wife and several children; another Italian, Morello, chartered the ship for the benefit of the dead man's heirs.

On November 18, 1907, the *Nueva Tigre* set sail from Callao for Pisco with a cargo of sulfate of potassium and coke. Both the captain, Nicolas Melis, and his mate, Jessen Boster, were Italian. The crew consisted of Skerrit and Mortelman.

The *Nueva Tigre* was never seen again, nor were Melis or Boster. On the other hand, the schooner which had left Callao with the name *Nueva Tigre* was the same ship that went aground on the reef at Apamama with only Mortelman and Skerrit, alias Taylor and Jackson, on board. The *Nueva Tigre* was now the *White Rose*.

What had happened to Melis and Boster? It was Skerrit who described their fate: At about 11 o'clock on the morning of their departure from Callao, the schooner was a good fifteen miles from the coast, making way under a steady breeze. Mortelman was at the helm, the mate on watch preparing a meal, Skerrit in the forward berth, and the captain asleep in his bunk. Hearing a terrible scream, Skerrit rushed out in time to see the mate running forward bleeding copiously from a gash in his neck. Mortelman was standing near the cabin, a bloody cleaver in his hand. At this point, Melis, the captain, appeared, and Mortelman struck him on the head with the cleaver, causing him to fall over backwards. In the struggle that followed, Melis managed to escape; Mortelman followed him, changed his mind, and returned to the cabin for his gun. Aiming it at the captain, he told him to throw himself into the sea. Melis grabbed a hatch cover and leaped over the bulwark with his improvised raft. Mortelman pulled the trigger, but the gun failed to go off. So the unfortunate captain was left to his watery fate and never seen again. As for the wounded mate, he managed to find refuge in the foresail's luff. He pleaded with Mortelman to let him come down, but the latter kept his gun trained on him. The poor man was losing so much blood that it was all over the sail and he was growing weaker by the minute. He finally slid down and fell into the water where he struggled for a few moments, then disappeared.

Terrified by this scene of horror, Skerrit waited his turn to be the next victim, but as it turned out, the pirate needed him to clear the blood off the deck. Then Mortelman ransacked the cabin, found the papers, logbook and the captain's effects, tied them into a bundle and threw them overboard. That done, he went to bed until it was his turn to take the watch, exactly as if nothing had happened.

The next days were spent throwing the cargo into the sea—a slow process—and painting the hull white (it had previously been green). They changed its name, and as it had only been painted on the stern, it was easy enough to scratch off and paint *White Rose* over it.

Their navigation was at best approximate, neither of them knowing how to fix a position. Mortelman thought that if they headed west, they would eventually reach

Australia, where they would have no difficulty selling the ship.

All that remained was to solve the problem of the ship's papers. Mortelman wrote up a deed of sale, dated October 3, 1907, Valparaiso, reinstating the name *Puelche* as on the wheel. But instead of writing it in Spanish as he should have done, he wrote it in English—and bad English at that, for its author was short on education. To give the document an air of authenticity, Mortelman thought he had just the thing when he came across a receipt-stamp in the captain's drawer. Unfortunately, the stamp was Peruvian instead of Chilean, as it should have been for a paper drawn up in Valparaiso.

To cap this series of aberrant falsifications, Mortelman took it into his head to sail under British colors, so he made up a Union Jack out of the various remnants of flags he found on board. The result was pure fantasy, bearing little resemblance to the British jack.

Eventually, Mortelman and Skerrit were transferred to Suva, seat of the Fiji government and its criminal court. Contacts with the Peruvian government confirmed Skerrit's recital, at least in so far as it concerned the identities of the captain, mate and schooner.

Gilchrist Alexander, a British magistrate, went to Callao in person to complete the investigation as ordered by the prosecutor in Fiji. But because of the distance involved, the Peruvian court returned the case to British justice and therefore it was before the criminal court in Suva that Mortelman was summoned to appear.

Mortelman took himself very seriously and played the role of pirate to the hilt. To everyone's surprise, he was not sentenced to death but only to life imprisonment. In spite of the conclusive evidence, British justice felt it could not mete out capital punishment in view of the impossibility of recovering the bodies.

V

~~~~~~

It was through an article in the *Daily Telegraph* of Sydney, brought by the *Richmond* on July 7, 1893, that Papeete learned of the drama that had taken place on the *Niuroahiti*. After the first expressions of astonishment came the chorus from the local wiseacres: "Didn't I tell you," "I was right after all," "If people had only listened to me," "Those boys were too polite to be honest," etc., etc.

The *Messager de Tahiti*, which carried the orotund slogan "Fluctuat pro Tahiti semper," published a special edition emblazoned with the boldest headlines at its disposal: HORRIBLE TRAGEDY! PIRACY IN THE PACIFIC! SEXTUPLE ASSASSINATION!

The editor's grandiloquent style seemed to imply that Papeete was a large city where the population knew nothing of the affair. In point of fact, the *paraparau*—the gossips of the market place—had exhausted the subject before the morning was out. The *Messager de Tahiti* was soon forced to find something new to whet its subscribers' appetites. Passing all too readily from fact to insinuation, it printed the following article: "A person employed in a highly respectable company, the first mate on the schooner which took the Roriques to Rarotonga, attended many parties with them in Papeete. He even gave them a map of the Caroline Islands. When the ship arrived at Papeete, the captain came ashore with members of the crew, and that very night, the two brothers suggested to the first mate that they take possession of the ship and set sail. Had the first mate been an honest man, he would have told the captain immediately instead of amusing himself in the brothers' company." So it came to pass that anyone who had anything to do with the Roriques became suspects and even accomplices. The finger was pointed at Wohler because he had had the misguided idea of bringing the brothers to Tahiti, not to mention Nagel, who "took part in their evenings on the town." And what of André who held Joseph in such high esteem, not to mention his wife? . . . But that vein could not be mined further, for Lucie fell ill during the month of January and was shipped back to France. Hospitalized while waiting for a boat to Sydney, she died on March 8 at the very moment that Joseph was being put in irons on the *Don Juan de Austria*.

Governor Lacascade, a native of the Antilles—the "negro" as Gauguin had labeled him—sent a report to the minister for the Colonies in a letter dated July 12. In it, he informed the minister that the public prosecutor in Papeete had begun an investigation.

Auguste Goupil, appointed lawyer for the defense, was a brother-in-law of William Gibson, the unfortunate supercargo on the *Niuroahiti*. He advised the widow, Teihotua a Tauraa, to bring the case into civil court, for he was under the impression that it would be tried in Papeete. The governor had already filed the formalities for extradition with the authorities in Manila. What was not known in Papeete was that a sextuple assassination was not within the jurisdiction of a court of common law but must be tried by a very special jurisdiction—the First Naval Tribunal in Brest.

Actually, the Rorique case fell within the provisions of Article 4 of the Law of April 10, 1825, which concerned crimes of piracy committed on the high seas. True, the cases judged by this court were infrequent, but some had had considerable repercussions. One of the most recent had involved the *Foederis Arca*, a brig carrying army provisions from Sète to Veracruz during the Mexican War, on which the crew, on June 29, 1864, had assassinated the captain and his mate in a most atrocious manner in order to take possession of the ship. Four sailors were denounced by the ship's boy, sentenced and guillotined in Brest on June 7, 1866.

After having informed the French government of the Rorique case, the Spanish authorities soon received a request from Paris to extradite the brothers into the custody of the First Naval Tribunal. And so the authorities in Manila now had a second demand for extradition. Should the Roriques go to France or Tahiti? The fact that the correspondence of the Governor of the Philippines had to go by way of Madrid did not help speed things up, and many months passed before a solution was found.

Meanwhile, the investigation was proceeding in Papeete where the brothers' identity became the central issue. Were they French as they appeared to be, or were they Canadian,

Australian, American, or in fact South African, as they claimed?

At this point, the chief of Postal Services in Tahiti turned over to the public prosecutor a letter from the dead-letter office addressed to Alexander in Kaukura and returned to Papeete stamped "Address Unknown." At first glance, the letter appeared to be written in some Nordic language. Hoppenstaed, director of the Société Commerciale de l'Océanie, and also German consul, thought it might be Dutch. By a stroke of luck, a Dutch ship happened to be in port with a cargo of California lumber. The officers on board examined the letter but did not understand it, although they occasionally caught the general meaning of certain sentences. Could it be Flemish? In the end, it was Leonard von der Labbe, a young clerk on board, who stated: "No, it's a dialect spoken on the border between Holland and Belgium. I know because I happen to come from there."

The letter had been written by Joseph while he was on the *Henry* to his brother at Kaukura. It had never reached its destination. The translation, worked out by the young clerk, read:

Dear Alex:

I arrived Sunday the 15th. We had a very good trip with a big cargo. I got your two letters. I don't know if we're going to Kaukura, but we might. In any event, be ready. See if you can cut out some letters for the name of the boat—from the tin of cracker boxes, for instance. I'm getting along well with André, but as soon as he arrives in Kaukura, we'll do it all the same.

I had a big laugh one night. There was a strong wind blowing and we were running under full sail. I was damned if I was going to take in an inch of sail. Our two passengers were praying on their knees [the Verbiziers] and the old man [André] asked me if I was trying to send him flying through his cabin porthole.

The old man wears out his shoe leather telling everybody in Tahiti that I'm the best mate anywhere near Papeete and everybody at the Société Commerciale is very nice to me. We spent five days beating around Anaa and the old man didn't come aboard day or night the whole time! But for two days, we sailed with two reefs in the mainsail, one in the foresail and the jib furled. The whaleboat capsized and I had to send three men into the water to save her and the copra. I was able to pick them up later. The old man was on land watching and told me later he'd been shaking like a reed!

The *Henry* is a damn good ship and never balks at coming about. We have only one set of sails on board. I'm doing everything I can to get another set. I'm trying to get everything I need so that I'll be able to do what's necessary. If we should be coming to Kaukura, I'll try to send you another letter before I leave, but I'll only be able to say that we're arriving on such and such a day, so that nobody will guess anything if the letter arrives too late. Be patient and keep up your courage; if it isn't this month, it'll be the next, because the trips never last more than a month.

André is leaving after the New Year and then I think Chemin will be captain. You remember the drunk we had in our room when we were with the four women and four men, and he pulled off his jersey to catch one of us, he didn't care which one. You'd have a good laugh if we turned up together again. But keep in mind where we'd be going if we talked too much.

One thing is certain, we can't last long without a crew, for it's a big boat and all the tackle is heavy to handle.

My clap is cleared up, I had just enough pills left to get rid of it. I hope yours is cured too. Give my regards to Richmond and Petterson. Especially Richmond: André said Richmond had joked with him a lot before I was taken on, saying I was such a good sailor. And now, gentleman, until later on! I send greetings from André, Andron and his wife—the redhead stinks like a black whore—and from Wohler and the thirty-six other jackasses.

Joe.

Except for this incriminating letter, the investigation by the public prosecutor in Tahiti turned up nothing more, especially where it concerned the brothers' identity. No one doubted that they were French. Wily old Captain Garnier noted that the hammocks the Roriques slept in were similar to the ones convicts used on the ships that transported them to New Caledonia. But an investigation into this possibility came to nothing: no escaped convicts from that *bagne* answered to the Roriques' description.

Meanwhile, Mirey had written a letter from his cell in the Casa Privilegia at Billibid to his master and owner of the *Niuroahiti*, Prince Hinoi. No one knows if this letter ever reached him. But the Prince did receive a letter from Mirey in June 1893. It was translated into French, with all its peculiar expressions and biblical allusions borrowed from the missionaries intact:

To Prince Hinoi:

    Greetings to you and everyone in your house, through the Mercy of our Lord, Jesus the Messiah, the real Saviour.

My master,

This is the second letter I've written to let you know of the terrible thing that happened on your ship. I wrote you the first time when we were jailed in the Manira [Manila] prison so that you would know everything I told the Spanish Governor. I mailed my first letter when we arrived in Ponape, Caroline Islands, on the twenty-seventh of May, eighteen hundred and ninety-two; since then I've waited until the new year eighteen hundred and ninety-three. And I haven't received an answer to my letter yet. That's why I thought I'd write you a second letter, thinking the first never reached you, since I never received an answer.

My dear master, don't be shocked, don't be angry with me. I tried by every means to save my life and your property. It's possible you're angry with me. Please don't think ill of me, I did my best to save your property as much as possible even though I was in mortal fear of them. My master, if God sees fit to prolong my days, I'll see you all again and tell you how much I suffered from that day to this, January sixteen, eighteen hundred and ninety-three.

I'm still in prison, wondering what fate has in store for me that I don't know about.

The French Consul came to see me on January seventh, eighteen hundred and ninety-three, and told me that a letter had arrived for me but he didn't tell me what was in it, and he also told me a letter from the governor at Tahiti had come, he also told me that he was waiting for orders from France and until then he wouldn't know if we were to be sent to Tahiti or France. He also told me that he was looking for a captain and sailors to take the ship back to Tahiti.

That's all he said to me. When he left, he gave me six piasters for me to buy some clothes, because I am in great need, having no pants, no shoes; I had nothing to buy them with. All I could do was submit to fate, hoping that the day

would come when the Lord would help me out of the difficulties I found myself in, trying to protect your property.

That's all I have to say, my dear master; say hello to Rovaru
Vahine [Princess Joinville], to Paraita, Hamaï, Paï and to
everybody of the house and all of our dear friends. That's all,
I close my letter with eyes full of tears when I think of Tahiti,
the land where I was born.

That's all, I greet you in the name of the true God forever
and ever.

Your affectionate servant, Terepahi or Hippolyte Mirey.

Say hello also to Antoni, Monsieur Cape.

And, if you would be so kind, my master, answer my letter
to relieve my mind.

Good-bye, my friend.

At almost the same moment, Tahiti was stunned by the
extraordinary news that both the Roriques and Mirey had
been condemned to death and executed by the Spanish
authorities in Manila.

The *Messager de Tahiti* published in full an article that
had appeared in the *San Francisco Chronicle*, quoting an
interview with a lady passenger on board the steamship
Rio de Janeiro which had stopped off in Manila at that
very moment.

With loving detail, the lady reported on the preparations for the execution, noting that the Rorique brothers
had watched the scene with stoicism, seeming to be less
interested than the spectators in what was going on. She
described how soldiers stood in a double line around the
area where the execution was to take place, holding back
the thousands who had come to watch the spectacle.

The cook shook with terror while the magistrate delivered the sentence; the executioner knocked him down with a slap on the face, then placed him on the block. Stepping back to give himself room, the executioner swung his sword and, bringing it down with the speed of lightning, severed the cook's head. The body fell in a heap and the head rolled a few feet in a gush of blood.

Then the Roriques, both tall and muscular men, were brought forward and forced to their knees. Their powerful sunburned necks were going to offer more resistance. Each pirate was held by two men. The executioner made a mark on each of the brothers' necks, then he had his aides step back. For a second time, the sword of the Law rent the air and fell with brutal force on the first neck, the head rolling toward the cook's. Then the second head fell.

Full of moral indignation, the lady concluded with the observation that these brutes who had cared so little for the lives of their fellow men had now met their own end, and that they were all the more guilty for being well educated and speaking a dozen languages, which indicated that they had once been members of a refined society.

There was not a shred of truth in the account. It was all pure invention and a hoax—all of which came to light almost immediately.

It should be noted, however, that the public viewed Mirey as a coward, and the brothers as murderers certainly, but murderers endowed with unusual courage. This opinion was reinforced as time went by.

The same issue of the *Messager de Tahiti* stated that "these two adventurers, who claimed to be Belgian, had used similar tactics to make off with a cutter loaded with copra." This was the Jaluit episode that Narrhum had reported in Ponape. But where did this claim of Belgian nationality, not heretofore mentioned, originate? It must have come from the same source, namely, from Narrhum's allegations.

If Mirey was receiving preferential treatment at Billibid, he was also beginning to fret over the interminable delay in the proceedings for his extradition. For surely the Roriques would be using this time to plan their escape, and Mirey was well aware of the danger to his life if that was successful.

With an astuteness surprising in a man usually given to lethargy, Mirey saw to it that the brothers were kept under tight surveillance. As a consequence, they were caught trying to escape from Billibid on two separate occasions: the first time, with an order for release they had drawn up themselves, using a purloined official seal—they were becoming specialists at this; the second time, they seized the weapons of the guards charged with their surveillance. These attempts earned them three months in the prison dungeon.

Finally, on March 7, 1893, they were shipped to Saigon on the German steamship *Ingrahan*, together with Mirey and the two sailors, Baka and Korotu, the third having died of dysentery during his incarceration in the Manila prison.

All the men were handcuffed and put in steerage, but as Joseph later said: "Any officer in the merchant marine who doesn't know how to open irons without a key is a fool." So, in no time, the brothers were out of handcuffs. It is easy enough to believe Joseph when he said: "Mirey's face, already terror-stricken to the point of decomposition, went green at the sight." It must have taken an extraordinary effort on their part not to take revenge on the cook. But had they given in to their instinct, it would certainly have meant the death sentence without appeal.

They disembarked in Saigon six days later, where they were turned over to the French authorities. Alexander was put in irons in the cell for those sentenced to death; Joseph was chained to an iron bar in a subterranean dungeon buzzing with mosquitoes. There they stayed two weeks. Then they set sail for Toulon on the navy transport *Shamrock*. This particular vessel had been built to serve as hospital ship and troop transport for the Tonkin War. Like the ancient ships, it had a double row of portholes, making it possible to ventilate the ship in good weather. Rigged with three masts including a square sail, it had a steam engine and was almost as unmaneuverable under steam as sail.

For the Roriques, the *Shamrock* was the worst penance they had ever endured. Since they knew what lay in store for them, they were expected to resort to the most reckless and desperate measures of escape. Therefore the crew was under strictest orders to see that the brothers were always in chains and under constant surveillance. It wasn't only that they had to be transported to France; they had to be delivered alive. Why then were they placed in a kind of lion's cage, a dungeon less than six feet square, without light or air in the very bottom of the ship, where regulations forbade leaving any man more than twenty-four hours?

Chief petty officer Blanchard, the highest-ranking officer on board and in charge of discipline, exhibited the zeal of a prison guard. Now guards have the excuse of their per-

sonal safety and that of the establishment to which they are assigned. But this was hardly the case here: the Roriques at this point were only indicted, even though their guilt seemed evident enough and eventual punishment scarcely in doubt. But Blanchard took the law into his own hands. As Joseph later described it: "We were made to sit on the floor, and they shackled our right feet to an iron bar. Then they crossed our left legs over our right legs and placed our left feet in irons so that our crossed legs were kept about fourteen inches apart. That's called being chained 'English-style.' When they had finished with our legs, they grabbed our arms and pinned them behind us and placed handcuffs in the shape of a figure 8 around our wrists, which totally immobilized our arms." As a result of these refinements, within a few days the irons had worked their way into their swollen flesh, making every movement an agony. They spent twenty-eight days in this torture chamber, and only their youth, stamina and mutual encouragement made it possible to survive what no animal could have borne.

By the time they arrived in Toulon on April 24, 1893, they were at the end of human endurance. For forty-seven days, they hadn't washed, their hair and beards were filthy and unkempt, and they were still wearing the same pants and jerseys they had on when they left Manila. When they were brought up on deck, they shivered in the mistral, and the brilliant light and fresh air were such a shock after the clammy darkness of their dungeon that they fainted on the deck while the naval police hurriedly tried to remove their irons.

They were led to the naval prison in Toulon, where

they were finally able to wash in a basin of icy water. Having no change of clothes, they also washed their underwear, pants and jerseys. Two days later, a detachment of five policemen led by Brigadier Stagnaro came for the brothers, Mirey, Baku and Korotu, and transferred them to Brest. Two compartments in the train had been prepared for them. Each man was chained to one of his guards, these being relieved every four hours. They were not left alone for a moment.

They arrived in Brest on April 28. It was a cool spring day, and the group went by foot from the station to the naval prison at Pontaniou on the right bank of the Penfeld where the naval station was situated. A small crowd had assembled along the way, for the strange drama played out in the distant Pacific had excited considerable curiosity. The *Dépèche de Brest* covered their arrival and it was of course the brothers who attracted the most attention. People expressed surprise at how little the Roriques looked like criminals. These were two well-built and prepossessing young men and it was hard to imagine them coldly murdering the entire crew of a ship. Baku and Korotu, shivering in their bare feet, cotton pants, jerseys and straw hats, were objects of pity. It was Mirey who looked the most guilty in the public's eye.

The pathetic procession passed through the Porte Foy, down the rue Voltaire, across the Place du Château, then took the ramp that led down through the Porte Tourville into the arsenal. For sailors like the Roriques, it must have been exciting to see so many ships tied up on both sides of the Penfeld's embankments: Under the chateau's walls lay the *Melpomène,* a school ship for seamen, and one of the undisputed achievements of the last years of sailing ships; next to it, the elegant *La Résolue,* a corvette for naval instruction; opposite the headquarters of the Chiefs-of-Staff, the *Loire,* a transport for the New Caledonia run which, with its line of black and white portholes and poop-deck, evoked the ships of the early nineteenth century; a little further, the *Dubourdien,* a cruiser school ship, just back from a campaign in the Pacific where it had gone as far as Tahiti.

The fjord-like estuary was a scene of constant bustle, as barges, tugboats and tenders of all kinds steamed in every direction, their maneuvers punctuated by sharp toots and whistles.

On both banks, dark massive granite buildings recalling the days of Richelieu and Colbert rose one above the other. On the left bank, the long building of the Corderie was overshadowed by the now unused sinister bulk of the penitentiary, and above that, the many wings of the naval hospital. On the right bank, perched high on a rocky escarpment, stood the fleet's coaling station and in a cleft in the side of the cliff, the drydock of Salou, dominated in turn by the shipyards of the Plateau des Capucins.

The procession had to cross to the right bank, using a floating bridge whose parts separated to make way for passing ships. They then climbed a ramp behind the naval artillery shipyards, passed through the Porte Rouge and arrived at the faubourg of Recouvrance, the prison of Pontaniou being outside the walls of the military port. After going through a low door hollowed out of the high walls, the Toulon police turned their charges over to Compredon, the prison warden.

This was hardly the end the Roriques had imagined for themselves as they sailed about the atolls of the South Pacific.

VI

MARITIME JUSTICE was not one to dawdle: the very next day, on April 28, Vice-Admiral de la Jaille of the port admiralty gave orders to begin the interrogation. The assignment was entrusted to Captain Crespin, a commander close to retirement age who seemed ill chosen for the role except perhaps for his long-ago campaigns in the Pacific. His assistant for all questions relating to the law was a navy purser. This improvised magistrate had been taught the elements of the case and probably knew the tricks of the trade where an interrogation was concerned. To Crespin, however, the case seemed perfectly simple: the guilt of the accused was beyond the shred of a doubt. Only one litigious point remained: their identity.

It was obvious that the identity they claimed at the time of their arrest was pure fantasy. The question was partly answered when, at the start of the interrogation, the brothers dropped the names Toussaint and de Vernier and admitted to being Joseph and Alexander Rorique, born, as everyone knew, in the province of Natal in South Africa. One request had already gone out to the Natal authorities

through the French consul in Durban, in the hope of veri-
fying the assertions the brothers had made at the time they
left Papeete.

On their arrival at the prison of Pontaniou, the Roriques
had been separated and put in solitary confinement—a bit
late and of questionable value. As it turned out, the year
they had been detained together had allowed them plenty
of time to perfect the defense Crespin was about to be
confronted with.

He was never able to make them contradict each other,
and they sprang every trap he tried to set for them. When
the interrogating magistrate asked Joseph: "Was your
father married to your mother?" Joseph exploded: "Your
family may be in the habit of making bastards, but let me
inform you that my parents were respectable people and I
forbid you to ask any more questions of that nature. I
might forget I was in the presence of an old man." Joseph
added later: "The minute I spoke those words, he cleared
the court."

From the start, the interrogation was off on the wrong
foot. For one thing, Crespin was convinced that the
Roriques had escaped from a penitentiary, even though all
inquiries made in New Caledonia and Guiana proved
fruitless. Still not satisfied, he launched an investigation
in other countries. For this purpose, he had the brothers
photographed, but only when they had had their heads,
beards and mustaches shaved off. Besides, who, looking at
those bony faces, sunken eyes and scraggly necks, could
have recognized the spirited leaders of Tahiti cotillions?
Certainly no one in Papeete when the townspeople were
shown the disconcerting photographs.

The judiciary, however, had carefully kept two weapons in reserve: first, Mirey's deposition which it had never seen but whose contents it could guess at, and secondly, Joseph's damaging letter to his brother in Kaukura.

Both were asked: "What happened to Tehahe, Gibson, the four sailors and the passenger on board the *Niuroahiti?*" And to Alexander: "You embarked on the ship as a passenger. How come you turned up in Ponape as its captain?"

Their replies were astonishing. According to them, their disappearances were the result of a series of calamities under very unusual circumstances. Joseph's deposition gave his version of the events, his motivation obviously being to show up the prosecution's principal witness—Mirey—for a liar: "We set sail from Papeete on December fifteenth and reached Kaukura two days later. My brother had no idea I was on the *Niuroahiti*. When he came on board the following day, he was very surprised to find me there, thinking I was still on the *Henry*.

"His affairs were going so well that he was almost out of merchandise and had come on board to see if we had any. I introduced him to Gibson, but the supercargo told him he had nothing to spare. There wasn't much on the *Niuroahiti*, and what little there was was promised to different agents working for its owner, Prince Hinoi, one of the agents being in Kaukura.

"But Gibson was sympathetic to my brother's predicament, so he signed him on for as far as Fakarava, where he could pick up the schooner *Mateata* to take him to Tahiti for more goods. He could then return to Kaukura, which is what Alexander agreed to do.

"During the trip, he took Tehahe's watch because the captain was suffering from a swollen gland in his groin, probably venereal. One of the passengers ran into some friends in Fakarava and decided to get off. We were both invited to a party at the resident's. Alexander met a young widow there who wanted him to stay with her. The schooner for Tahiti had already gone, so the woman had no trouble persuading my brother to stay until the next boat came. To make it more pleasant for him, she decided to introduce me to one of her friends. On the way, she told me that her friend had a jealous husband and showed me a place where I could wait for her without being seen.

"I lay down in the grass and waited a long time. When nobody came, I decided it had been a practical joke and went back to the ship. That long wait in the damp grass gave me a chill. I went straight to my bunk, but during the night, I ran a high fever and the next morning I couldn't get up.

"Gibson was very upset, what with Tehahe's being ill and now the mate. He explained the situation to Alexander and how the *Niuroahiti*'s trip would take about a month, which was what he'd have to wait anyway until the *Mateata* returned. So Gibson said, why not go with us?

"Alexander accepted. The only problem was our nationality. Gibson said that in view of the emergency, he would take care of the matter. We set sail the following morning. Just before we left, two natives employed by the resident came on board to collect Alexander's belongings at the widow's request. They went back empty-handed.

"The reason I mention this woman is to make clear

that up to that point, my brother had no intention of staying on the *Niuroahiti*. I'm certain that if that had been his intention, he wouldn't have made the arrangements he did with the lady.

"From the start, Tehahe pretended he didn't know what Alexander's position was. He was jealous about his taking his own place. I think I was on good terms with the crew, at least when I was up and around, and anything Tehahe said to the men couldn't have had much effect on them. But with me bedridden, Tehahe—without meaning to, perhaps—prepared them for revolt. Tehahe was constantly inciting the crew against my brother, and Gibson often had to break up arguments.

"If I'd become captain, I don't think it would have bothered him, but he insisted on thinking of Alexander as a passenger. It was Tehahe's habit—his biggest concern on the ship, actually—to summon the crew to the stern and recite a prayer. The evening of the drama, he shouted even louder than usual: 'Te Atua, te Atua e—e—e—' to the point where my brother ordered him to lower his voice so that I wouldn't be disturbed.

"Tehahe tried to work on Gibson's sympathy, but failing that, he complained to the sailors and this laid the groundwork for what followed.

"During the night, we were supposed to sail past a certain island. My brother didn't go to bed, and in due course, he sighted the island up ahead. We were then on a starboard tack. Alexander tried to locate the island by compass, when it suddenly appeared in front of the ship. He turned around to give Farina, who was at the helm, a piece of his mind and saw that he was asleep. You don't take such things lightly on board ship, so he picked up a wet swab and swatted Farina in the face. The man woke up with a start, let go the tiller and rushed to the bow, shouting something in Tahitian.

"Alexander took the tiller, assuming that Farina would calm down and come back to apologize for his inexcusable negligence. But nothing happened. From the tiller, Alexander couldn't see the crew's quarters because the galley was between. But leaning to starboard, he could make out four sailors, one armed with a capstan bar, another with a hand pump, creeping toward the stern.

"Alexander jumped to the port side of the tiller and, reaching through the porthole near the head of my bunk, grabbed my revolver and thus armed, ordered the sailors to stop. As they continued to inch forward, he shot into the air. The bullet went through the top of the mainsail. This brought the sailors to a stop by the starboard pump.

"Tehahe was sleeping fully dressed on the roof of the deckhouse. The sound of the shot woke him up. He said something to the sailors, wheeled suddenly toward Alexander, took out his revolver and opened fire. His gun failed to go off; he tried again, but again it didn't go off. My brother aimed his at Tehahe; Tehahe threw his gun at Alexander's head. My brother ducked in time and the revolver fell behind the tiller.

"Thinking he was at Alexander's mercy, Tehahe jumped over the rail into the sea, yelling something to the sailors. My brother only caught the word 'fenua' [land] and concluded that out of desperation, the man was going to try to swim to the island—which was perfectly possible if he hadn't been half-crippled.

"Alexander rushed to the cabin companionway, pushed it open and yelled in English: 'Gibson, come up on deck. There's mutiny on board.' He was still holding his revolver and as he pushed open the hatch, it hit the recoil slide which tripped the trigger and released a bullet. The bullet skidded down the deck toward the port whaleboat. The men were on the starboard side and couldn't get over to port side because the whaleboat filled the space between the rail and the galley. So they retreated to the bow.

"Gibson had got his *pareu* tied around his waist and came on deck. I was also awake by then, but too weak to come to my brother's rescue. But what was that lazy bastard Mirey doing, lying on his bunk opposite me? The curtains were pulled almost closed, but I could just see his face frozen with fear. He was trembling so hard it made the curtains shake. At any other time, I would have laughed.

"I told him to go up on deck and give Alexander and Gibson a hand. I had heard Gibson calling out 'That's all right, that's all right!' after the boat had come about and heeled over on the starboard side. Then I heard a big thud. I could feel the impact below. My brother yelled and sounded very distressed about something. I summoned all the strength I had and got out of bed, but the minute I stood on my feet, I collapsed to the floor.

"Finally, Alexander ordered Mirey on deck. He told him to stay at the helm and warn him if anybody came near, then he came down to the cabin. He put me back to bed and told me what had happened. Before Gibson had come on deck, Alexander had already swung the ship to starboard so that the *Niuroahiti* would be between

[97]

Tehahe and the island where he could pick him up. He said: 'I couldn't count on the crew because they were in open revolt. But with the sails well sheeted in, I could put about without them. This way we'd drift toward Tehahe. When Gibson arrived, I told him briefly what had happened. He said: "That damned fool," and went on the starboard side of the deckhouse to see if he could locate Tehahe anywhere. The wind was putting enormous pressure against the mainsail. The halliard was too weak and gave way, the boom tackle broke loose and the wind swung the boom with savage force, hitting Gibson on the neck. He was thrown clear off the ship. I'm sure he was already dead from the blow.

" 'I saw or heard nothing more. I lunged at the big sheet to pull in the slack, but what could I do alone? An entire crew couldn't have held it. The wind tore it out of my hands, giving me a bad rope burn.' Beside himself with despair, my brother said:

" 'So what are we to do, my poor Joseph? We don't seem to have much luck. Things were just beginning to look good when all these troubles started raining down on us. What will they say in Tahiti? I'm in a pretty ambiguous position. I was a fool not to stay at Fakarava. And all this because of that idiot Tehahe. I'm sure he could reach land in spite of his ailment. But I could hardly jump in after him, leaving you here alone with a mutinous crew. How will we get to Tahiti? If you're not well soon, I don't know what I'll do. I can't hand over the deck and the ship's safety *and* your life to that idiot cook when I have to sleep? Who's to say he won't aid and abet those savages? What are we to do, Joseph, what are we to do?'

"We decided to cruise in the area for a while. When we'd given up all hope of finding the two men, we headed for Tahiti. Alexander stayed at the tiller as long as he was able. When fatigue finally overtook him, he helped me up on deck and laid me down on a bench near the tiller with a revolver so that I could keep an eye on the helmsman while he slept.

"He had already forbidden all the sailors to come aft except for the man on watch. At the first sign of disobedience, I was to fire my gun to wake him up. Mirey kept to his galley, saying he wasn't capable of taking the helm.

"The emotional strain of the last few hours had helped lower my fever, but I was still very weak. The most I could do was keep watch for my brother in case the sailors started to mutiny again. But gradually, the excitement and my determination gave me back my strength and I was able to take the watch regularly. That was on January seventh. My brother had gone down to rest when a sailor came to me and said the passenger was dead. He was actually laughing when he said it! I'm not likely to forget that.

"At first, under these circumstances, the news was such a shock that I couldn't quite take it in. I thought he was joking, but at the same time, I felt a spasm of terror and almost choked with the horror of it. I tried to find out more from the sailor without really knowing how to go about it. He couldn't give me any explanation. I shouted for Alexander and told him the news. He stormed and yelled and swore at the bad luck that was hounding us. Then he decided he wanted to see for himself.

"I advised him to take a weapon, for it had just occurred to me that perhaps this new death was a ruse to get my brother to the bow—an ambush to put Alexander at the sailors' mercy.

"The body was brought on deck. He was dead all right, but there didn't seem to be any explanation for it. It looked natural enough; no sign of violence, nothing that suggested a crime. Then we remembered that the poor man hadn't come on deck for several days. We hadn't attached much importance to the fact; being a passenger, he was free to do whatever he liked.

"We couldn't preserve the body until Tahiti, so we laid him down on the hatch cover and draped him with a flag. At noon, Alexander summoned the crew and told them to stand around the body. He read some passages from the Bible in their language, then the body was lowered into the sea. I sat at the tiller during the ceremony. The sailors were quiet and respectful. Only Mirey looked sullen. I was very sad about the man's death. Not only because I felt sorry for him, but because his death might mean even more trouble for us. How were we to explain his death? What would I say if someone asked me why I hadn't noticed he was sick?

"The sailors were very friendly with me. I guess I made a good impression on them. They liked me much better than my brother, not that he wasn't kind to them, but he was more distant, and Tehahe had gone out of his way to make him look bad to them.

"When I was on duty, the man at the helm often talked to me. Especially Pietau. He was always apologizing for himself and his friends and wondering what could have gotten into them to mutiny against us.

"I told him that certainly mutiny was severely punished,

especially when it caused a man's death, but as there had
been no crime—only accidents—I had no intention of letting my men be punished, and that everything would turn
out all right in the end.

"One day, Pietau asked me if it were true that the crew
could be sentenced to death. He said Mirey had told him
that. He begged me to persuade my brother to change
course and leave him and the other sailors off on one of
the islands in the group.

"I tried to convince him that he had nothing to fear,
and that the worst that could happen to him was a few
days in jail. I told him: 'My brother will certainly refuse
to drop you off anywhere but in Tahiti. And even if he
agreed to do it, I'd oppose it with all my might. Besides,
there's no island in the Pomotu where you'd be beyond
the law's reach.'

"When I told Alexander about this, he gave Mirey a
sound scolding and told him to please keep his foolish
nonsense to himself and stop frightening the natives.

"We were due to arrive in Tahiti during the night of
January ninth. My watch was from midnight to four.
Around eleven-thirty, my brother sighted land, heaved to,
and went down to the cabin to examine the map. The
noise he made woke me up. I asked him: 'Is it my watch
already?'

" 'No, not yet,' he said. 'You still have a half hour. But
I want you to get up. I need your help. I think it's Tetiaroa
I see straight ahead and it should be to the northwest.'
Tetiaroa is an atoll about thirty miles north of Papeete.

"For four days we'd been sailing with a following wind
slightly to starboard, and right away we wondered if the

sailors at the helm had been heading her up imperceptibly. We weren't convinced yet that they'd done it on purpose. Maybe it was just a matter of luck or some fluke. Anyway, we immediately decided to come about; we could still make Tahiti by sunrise.

"Mirey had meanwhile come on deck. My brother shouted for the men to make the maneuver. There was no answer. When he called again and still no one answered, he asked Mirey to go to the bow and see what the men were up to. He came back a few moments later and said that nobody was there, that he had called into the crew's quarters with no result and there was no light in the bow.

"Alexander wanted to go see for himself, but I was always afraid of an ambush and told him to take a gun and lantern. Mirey was ordered to light the lantern and took a good ten minutes to do it. Together they searched the quarters, but they were empty. There was a passageway between the forecastle and the hold, but my brother was afraid to risk going through the narrow opening, so he closed it from the forecastle side and returned to the deck.

"He went down to the hold by way of the hatch, taking Mirey with him, but again, no one was there. The whaleboat was on the port side of the deck rail. As they came up from the hold, Mirey raised his lantern, peered into the boat and announced that an oar was missing.

"I'd been observing Mirey ever since the mutiny, and his behavior often made me suspicious. A thought now crossed my mind. It was still only a vague suspicion, but I wondered if that half-breed had had reasons for not coming up on deck with Gibson, that he'd had reasons for being cynical when we lowered the passenger's body into the sea, and here again, that he'd had reasons for going to the bow as soon as he knew land had been sighted.

"I asked him straight out how many oars were supposed to be in the whaleboat; he stuttered something, but of course he had no idea. He guessed, however, that the men had swum to Tetiaroa, which was easy enough for natives, and that probably Farina with his game foot had taken the oar to help keep him afloat.

"I didn't argue with him because I didn't want to provoke my brother. If he shared my suspicions, he wouldn't have taken it as coolly as I did. Alexander was usually a calm man but he was beginning to lose his head.

"We could have stayed near Tetiaroa. The island wasn't very big, but what else was there to do? We could have got the whaleboat into the water after much effort, but who could have rowed it, since one of us had to stay on the ship to sail her? Then what would we have done with the whaleboat? Leave Mirey in it while the other man went looking for the natives? Impossible! One lone man can't force four men into a boat against their will!

"My advice was to head straight for Tahiti. It was the only solution. Mirey's dull brain came up with a thousand reasons why we shouldn't. He explained that Tetiaroa was uninhabited. Twice a year only, men were sent to gather coconuts and make copra. The men used whaleboats and canoes which they left on the island. The mutineers were probably on their way to Tahiti this very moment, and would certainly reach it before we did. Those men knew what their mutiny was exposing them to. You can be sure they'd agreed among themselves on how to explain the event, and we were certain to be arrested on arrival for, to avoid punishment for their mutiny, they'd probably say we had killed Gibson and maybe also Tehahe.

"Alexander was perplexed. Half crazy from the succession of misfortunes, he was beset with all kinds of fears. He saw himself faced with a series of intractable problems. What could he say? He wasn't even registered and Gibson was no longer around to vouch for him.

"Mirey had the effrontery to say that it would be very dangerous for Alexander to go back to Tahiti. 'Joseph,' he said, pointing to me, 'has nothing to fear. He's on good terms with the sailors, but you, Alexander, they don't know you, they don't recognize you as their boss, and you know that you can't reason with a crowd, especially when it's a crowd of natives.'

"I argued as best I could. I brought up every argument I could think of to counter Mirey's advice. But, alas, to no avail. Alexander's confidence was shaken; for the first time in his life, he was frightened. He didn't dare return to Tahiti.

"I argued that the natives weren't as bad as people said, that there were police and gendarmes and soldiers if we needed protection . . . At that, Mirey spoke up: 'Protect you! That won't keep you from going to prison all the same, while they conduct their investigation.' Then he added: 'Once you're in there, I know from experience you don't get out so easily, and you leave a few feathers behind. . . .'

"At the time, we didn't know that Mirey was an habitual

offender and that he had two convictions for theft and dealing in stolen goods to his credit.

"It was hopeless. Mirey had convinced my brother. Alexander asked me to take him someplace that wasn't French and that had communications with either Australia or America. Once there, meaning in a safe port, he'd wait and see what happened. As for me, I could take on a new crew wherever I left him off and bring the *Niuroahiti* back to Tahiti.

"Mirey agreed heartily. My chief argument against it was the harm it would do the owner of the ship. Mirey broke in: 'There's no reason you can't be doing business all the while. All you have to do is give the owner an exact reckoning. Officially, you're the supercargo in Gibson's place. Who's to say whether you make him more money this way than if the trip had ended in the Tuamotus?'

"Since my brother was leaning in this direction, I had to give in, although it was against my better judgment. And if I may say so, it was the only mistake I made. But it took two of us to do it. If we didn't return to Tahiti, what then? Where should we go? Go south toward Australia? That was out of the question. Much too far and the return trip would be much too difficult. Go east? Nothing there. North? Nothing there either. West? The Samoan islands. It was a good area, it appealed to my brother, but it would mean a difficult return sailing into a head wind.

"In the end, we decided on the island of Sydney and set our course in that direction. Our fate was sealed.

"I don't really remember if we became aware that the ship's papers were missing before or after the desertion. I think it must have been before, and that it was one of the

reasons why my brother decided not to go to Tahiti. I
know people are going to make every effort to track them
down, but it's useless. All they'll find is the tin box which
once contained them. We assumed they'd been left with
the resident at Fakarava when Tehahe presented them for
inspection, or that he had them on him when he jumped
off on the night of the fifth. We had to have regulation
papers to enter any country. Because of our awkward situation, my brother had the idea of making up some temporary papers to avoid future trouble. We had nothing to
print with on board, and it would look strange to have
handwritten papers if we were keeping the name *Niuroahiti* and Papeete our home port. So my brother chose
Rarotonga, and we changed the ship's name to *Poe*, the
name of the schooner we'd been offered at Rarotonga.
Since all this was temporary, we didn't even try to scratch
the painting off. We removed the lead letters from the
transom and from *Niuroahiti—Papeete*, we made up *Poe—
Avarua*, which is why the old letters were still clearly
visible under the new. This fact was noted by the Spanish
authorities. As soon as I'd left my brother off, all I'd have
to do was replace the old letters and I was ready to return,
for we hadn't destroyed the French flag nor the four for
the international code that made up the *Niuroahiti*'s name
and home port.

"A few days later, we came within sight of the island of
Sydney, but all our signals were in vain. The only answer
we got was the raising of the British flag. No canoe, no
boat came near us. We were forced to go to Hull. We
spent a whole day there making futile signals. That night,
we noticed a large number of torches the length of the

island. We learned later that these islands were at war.

"The wind having fallen, the current took us near the island of Peru. We were soon surrounded by canoes. A man from one of them came aboard and piloted us to our mooring. My brother went ashore. I was alone with Mirey and about twenty natives. There was a constant going back and forth between the ship and land.

"During the course of the day, I thought maybe the ship was dragging its anchor. I dived down to make sure it was well lodged. While I was thus occupied, there was nothing to prevent Mirey from informing on us.

"Alexander didn't return to the ship until evening. A white trader, a missionary, and a few natives came with him in two boats. Alexander told me that no mailboats stopped at the island, it had little traffic and no one knew when another ship might come by. He had hired three young natives who said they had already made the trip in a whaleboat. They were to help out until my brother left. We had to put in writing to the missionary that we would bring the men back to Peru on our return trip.

"If Mirey had seen the atrocities he accused us of, why didn't he say so here?

"During the night, we set sail for Apamama. As soon as we were under way, we could see that the three natives were worse than useless. They were more of a hindrance than a help. It was clearly the first time they'd ever set foot on a ship.

"We had contracted to bring them back on our return trip, but if we'd had the time, we would have turned around and got rid of them right away. As it was, we had three useless mouths to feed. It was impossible to teach them anything.

"At Apamama we ran into the American schooner *Equator*. We already knew Cameron, its captain. It had been chartered for a year by the writer Robert Louis Stevenson, and would be returning to America in a few months. Cameron assured us that a mailboat would soon be passing by Ebon. So we decided to go there.

"It was better to waste three or four more days than to leave my brother alone with natives for months. We'd gone through enough misery in Penrhyn to rid us forever of the desire to live on a flat coral island.

"The king of Apamama came on board and bought several things in exchange for copra. I didn't want my owner to take any more losses on account of the time we'd wasted. We got rid of as many perishables as possible, such as flour, rice, preserved foods, etc. As we were about to set sail, the king made a great fuss about a bottle of bitters that had been subtracted from his purchases. If we'd ever felt like shooting anybody, it was at that moment. The king went off in a rage, muttering threats. The Peru natives told us to be on our guard, for the Apamama natives would be attacking us that night.

"That took care of any desire to leave my brother there. We weighed anchor at daybreak and left. Before leaving, Cameron had invited us to stop at the island of Makin. He promised to fill up my hold with copra and at lower prices than in the Tuamotus. We gave him some merchandise and left the account open until we reached Makin. If we hadn't intended to come back, we wouldn't have left the money Cameron owed us behind.

"As we were leaving Apamama, Mirey proudly showed us the bottle of bitters he'd stolen from the king. He was soon sorry; we threw the bottle into the sea and gave him a good thrashing.

"When we reached Ebon, we learned that the packet boat had passed by two days before. As the *Niuroahiti*'s hull was very dirty, to the point where it was slowing us down considerably, we hired some divers to clean her. The cook made daily trips ashore to buy us provisions. There were several whites around, and any complaint lodged by Mirey would have got us arrested immediately.

On board ship, Mirey did only the cooking and laundry. He couldn't, or didn't want to learn to steer the ship. As we were about to weigh anchor, he told us that all our laundry was ashore and wouldn't be ready until evening. There were sharp words and he got another thrashing. As a result, we didn't leave until the next day. It didn't make sense for us to wait there for a mailboat that was irregular at best.

"One of the whites on the island promised me a quantity of copra when I returned. As we got ready to leave, the anchor's buoy caught in a mass of coral. We didn't wait to free it. We asked the white trader to keep it. We'd pick it up on our way back.

"Between Ebon and Kusaie, we ran into a big storm. When it came time to lower the flying jib, none of the natives dared go out on the bowsprit even though we'd heaved to. So I had to furl the sail myself. While I was doing that, a native loosed the jib, the ship immediately gathered way, and the waves came dashing over my head. It was a miracle I survived.

"Later, the pin fell out of the top halliard block of the mainsail. I climbed up, and in order to use both my hands, I had to sit in a hanging gadget sailors call a boatswain's chair. Since my brother was at the helm, Mirey let me down, but in his evil mood, he almost managed to drop me several times. Once safely on deck, I gave him a piece of my mind. He answered me insolently and we came to blows.

"There were no ships at Kusaie. The head wind at the passage kept us from leaving, so I made use of the time to restock our water supply. The three natives went with me. When we left Fakarava, we had water enough for a crew of ten for a month. With only six people, we'd used up the water in a few days. Only Mirey could have wasted it this way, to make things as difficult as possible for us. When I returned to the ship, Mirey was alone with a white trader and a crowd of natives. My brother was ashore.

"Here again, Mirey could have informed on us without risking anything. We were gone almost the whole day, and Kusaie is a large island, like Rarotonga.

"Some natives asked if they could go with us to Mac-Askyll, the first island in the Spanish Carolines. Since this island was on the way to Ponape where there was a regular mailboat, we took them on. As we arrived before Mac-Askyll, we were met by enormous whaleboats loaded with people. We had at least eighty natives, their king, a missionary and a white trader on board at all times. Again, what was Mirey waiting for? A single word to any one of these men and we would have been bound like sausages, if they hadn't killed us outright.

"We finally arrived at Ponape, but we'd missed the mailboat by two days. The extra day on Ebon, the bad weather and the time wasted at Kusaie had done it. This couldn't go on. My brother would have to wait here for the next packet. There was a Spanish village; he would get off here and I'd resume the trip to Tahiti by way of Ebon, Makin and Peru.

"We dropped anchor between a Spanish gunboat, the *Dona Maria de Molina*, and the Spanish torpedo cruiser, *Don Juan de Austria*. The port doctor came on board and gave us a clean bill of health.

"At noon, Alexander went ashore with the lifeboat. Since it had no sails, he took the three natives and Mirey. As soon as he reached the quay, several Spanish officers took him in hand—in a perfectly friendly manner—and stayed with him until he reached the governor's. The governor had him for dinner and kept him until evening. During this time, Mirey was wandering around the village —an ideal time to inform on us for the crimes he claimed to have witnessed.

"At the end of the day, everybody came back on board, very pleased with their visit ashore. I seem to remember that it was a Thursday. Alexander had already found a place to stay while he waited for the next mailboat. A German named Narrhum loaned him a mast and sails for the lifeboat.

"The next day, we were visited by numerous officers— both army and navy—several American, German and Spanish traders, and a large number of natives. There were always at least a dozen boats bobbing around the *Niuroahiti*, including launches from the *Dona Maria de Molina* and the *Don Juan de Austria*. Both launches were armed,

[111]

the island being in a state of siege. Why didn't Mirey inform on us then?

"On Saturday, a Tahitian woman who lived on the island came aboard. We exchanged a few words, and as other clients were arriving, we left her with Mirey. Again, he said nothing. That evening Alexander and I crossed the bay to visit a German who lived on that side. As we came back, we noticed that a boat was still tied up to the schooner. Mirey was in the cabin with a Spanish officer. Soon after, the officer left without having transacted any business. We warned him that we wouldn't be doing any more business from then on, the next day being Sunday and the *Niuroahiti* sailing on Monday morning.

"Another splendid occasion for the half-breed to denounce us! And even if he'd had none of these opportunities, there was one thing he could always do. We were moored between two warships. He had fifty yards to swim or traverse by boat to find asylum and denounce us to his heart's content. But he did nothing.

"Sunday we went ashore. Before reaching the village, we tied up at a German trader's pier to deliver an order left over from the day before. At this point, a very childish incident took place. Added to the various trials Mirey had undergone on the trip, I'm sure that was what made him decide to get his revenge.

"The German couldn't seem to get his siphon to work. Mirey, who had followed us with the merchandise, offered to help. The gadget had water in it and needed two different powders in certain proportions. Taking on the airs of a man of science, Mirey asked for a spoon and started to pour in first a spoonful of the first powder, then a spoonful

The Papeete waterfront in 1890. The San Francisco mailboat *Tropic Bird* is moored near the Societé Commerciale de L'Océanie.

Little Poland Street in Papeete. Renvoyé's restaurant is at the left of the lady in white.

Right: Papeete about 1890. A party at the United States Consulate, a California "brake" stationed in front.

A Papeete store about 1895, with policemen, personnel and customers grouped in front.

Right: The Tahitian press announces the news of the drama on July 9, 1892.

Supplément au N° 415 du 9 Juillet 1892

MESSAGER DE TAHITI

TE VEA NO TAHITI

MONITEUR HEBDOMADAIRE DES INTÉRÊTS COLONIAUX FRANÇAIS

PARAISSANT LE SAMEDI

PRIX D'ABONNEMENT

Un an, 25 fr. — Six mois, 13 fr. 50 — Trois mois, 7 fr. 50

Les abonnements sont payables d'avance. — On ne continue pas par réclamation.

Tout ce qui concerne le Journal doit être adressé franco au siège de l'Administration

RUE DU MARCHÉ, À PAPEETE, TAHITI

Les écrits anonymes ne sont pas insérés.

Les Annonces pour la France sont reçues au siège de
l'Association de la Presse Coloniale, 3, rue Drouot, Paris

TARIF DES INSERTIONS

Publications en première page (la ligne) .... Fr. 2.50
Faits divers-Réclames (2e page),   d° .... 1 fr.
Annonces (3 col. à la page),   d° 0.50
Annonces répétées,   d° 0.25

On traite à forfait pour les annonces à l'année

HORRIBLE TRAGÉDIE !

PIRATERIE DANS LE PACIFIQUE ---- SEXTUPLE ASSASSINAT

Affaire de la "NIUROAHITI"

Papeete in 1895. The small black-hulled schooner anchored near the hangers at the upper right is the *Niuroahiti*. Right: Seen closer-to while it was sequestered.

Prince Hinoi, nephew of King Pomare V and owner of the *Niuroahiti,* in the uniform of a cavalry officer.

The amiable Queen Makéa of Rarotonga, taken about 1890.

Hippolyte Mirey, the cook aboard the Niuroahiti and principal witness for the prosecution.

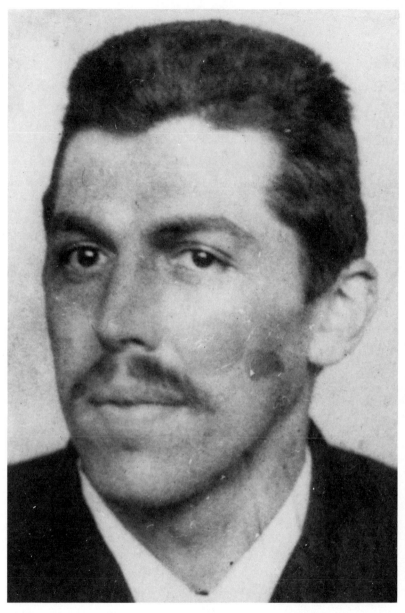

Eugène Degrave, at the time of the trial in December 1893.

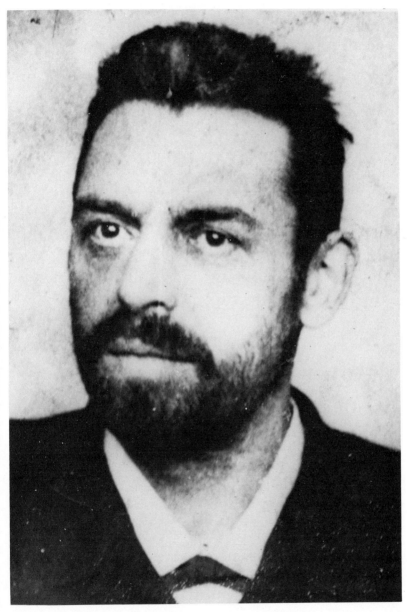

Léonce Degrave, bearing a striking resemblance to his brother, when the trial in Brest was underway.

Eugène Degrave as he looked in his police photograph taken at the time of his incarceration in Brest.

Léonce Degrave, his police photograph before the start of the trial in Brest.

Eugène Degrave, alias Joseph Rorique, uniformed and bemedalled before his ill-fated adventures in the South Seas.

Léonce Degrave, alias Alexander Rorique, wearing the medals given him by the Kings of Norway and Belgium for his acts of bravery in the North Sea.

The steamer *Navua,* which brought the Spanish flu to the South Pacific, moored in Papeete on November 16, 1917.

San Francisco in 1917. The intersection of Market and Powell Streets with a cable car taking on passengers.

of the second, to the point where the siphon exploded in his hands.

"The German's anger was beyond description. Invective and grief poured out of him. He screamed and yelled, cursing Mirey for his clumsiness and ended up demanding that he pay for the siphon.

"Mirey spoke heatedly in his own defense, saying he had only tried to be useful, that it wasn't his fault if there'd been an accident, and moreover the siphon, the German and everything else could go to hell.

"The discussion was getting out of hand, and Alexander and I decided we had to do something. I suggested my brother be the mediator, and he accepted after asking if either party objected, which they did not.

"Alexander came up with the following solution: that Mirey was wrong to get mixed up in something that didn't concern him, and the German was wrong to hand his siphon over to a clumsy fool. Therefore, the damage was to be shared. It was a fair decision. The German agreed. Mirey, however, went white with rage. He gnashed his teeth, rolled his eyes and announced he had no intention of complying: 'I won't pay a sou!'

"This upset my brother and he said to Mirey: 'All right then, Joseph will take it out of your wages.'

"Mirey looked Alexander straight in the eye and said: 'We'll see about that!'

"The hour had come for our informer to set about his dirty work. Even though the incident of the siphon appeared to be of little account, I'm convinced it played a part in Mirey's next step.

"Once in the village, we gave Mirey and the natives the

day off. Alexander and I made a tour of the village and he had me meet the two white sailors he had hired for the return trip. They seemed very happy to have found a ship and promised to be on board the next morning. They were hired for as far as Tahiti.

"Toward evening, we went to a public house where a Spanish sailor was playing the accordion. I recognized it at once as my own. I asked the sailor how he had come by it. He said he'd bought it for next to nothing from Mirey when he'd come aboard the previous evening with the Spanish officer. Perhaps this wasn't all Mirey had stolen. We started to look for him. After a while, I saw him walking, half drunk, into Narrhum's—the man who had loaned us the sail for the lifeboat. Mirey was staggering, his eyes bleary and bulging, his big hat at a cockeyed angle.

"I accosted him and asked: 'Did you steal my accordion? Answer me!'

"My surprise attack sobered him up, his eyes glistened, but his natural shiftiness took over. With a cringing smile on his stupid face, he replied: 'Your accordion! I sell your accordion? Come on! It must be on board where you last left it.'

"I wasn't taken in by this ruse and said: 'That makes it very simple. Let's go back to the ship together. You know where I always keep it and you give it to me.'

"Mirey saw he was outsmarted. He lost his assurance and became threatening, shouting: 'I go back to the ship! I go back to your miserable schooner! I will not! And that isn't all. You pay me a thousand piasters this very minute and let me have my belongings, or I go straight to the authorities and tell them you killed Gibson.'

"I suddenly saw through the man's attempt at black-mail; I lunged at him and gave him a thousand piasters' worth of blows. Narrhum came out on his veranda, and seeing two men fighting below, let go with a powerful kick. He was on a level with my head and I caught it right in the eye.

"I couldn't see for the blood pouring down my face and Mirey got away. My brother had seen Narrhum's cowardly act and came to square accounts. He gave the German a thrashing and the man started to yell. In no time, we were surrounded by a Spanish patrol who wanted to take us to the police station. In spite of their bayonets, we refused to go, so they decided to take us to the governor.

"The governor refused to see us but gave orders to re-lease us immediately and asked that we explain ourselves— or rather, lodge our complaint—the next morning. We asked that Mirey be returned to the ship. For a considera-tion of ten piasters, Captain Aguilar of the 69th Philipinas saw that he was brought before us. Mirey gave us back the key to the storeroom but refused pointblank to go aboard the ship. Aguilar told us not to worry. As the island was in a state of siege, Mirey would inevitably be picked up in the streets after eight o'clock and returned to us in the morning in time to set sail.

"We went aboard about seven o'clock with the three natives. Since we'd never paid much attention to the cook-ing, we forgot about the men's supper. In their simple-minded way, they thought their meals were a daily present from Mirey. They'd never received any food from our hands, so it didn't occur to them to ask us for it. They waited until we were in bed and when the cook hadn't come back, they swam ashore.

"The Spanish sentinels stationed along the water's edge saw them and started shooting. The men weren't hit, but as soon as they reached land, they were arrested and taken to the police station where Mirey was.

"One of the Spaniards who spoke a little French had witnessed the fight at Narrhum's and heard Mirey's threats. He now asked him to explain what he meant when he said: 'I'm going to tell them you killed Gibson.' He recognized our natives and started to question them, but the men understood only the language of Peru and a few English and French words they had picked up on the ship. The Spaniard understood only 'captain,' 'mate,' 'boat' and the natives' imitation of the sentinels' motions and the sound of their guns going 'put-put-put.' The officer decided the men were confirming what he'd gleaned from Mirey's account, so he informed the governor, and the governor gave orders for our arrest the next morning at dawn.

"Before going to bed, my brother and I discussed our situation. It was obvious we were in a tight spot. We'd done enough sailing in Spanish waters to know the greed of Spanish officials; it was legendary among all sailors. The schooner and especially its contents were all too likely to disappear into the pockets of Ponape's officialdom.

"What should we do? We could escape easily enough. We had only to set the sails, weigh anchor and leave. There were two outcroppings of coral to be avoided, but we knew exactly where they were. We'd been sailing the *Niuroahiti* alone for a month and handling the ship had become second nature. And even if we were afraid about getting out of the port, we could always abandon the ship and load up the whaleboat with mast, sails, provisions, our belongings, and disappear.

"The Spaniards were despised in the group of islands we were in. Any native would have given us asylum because we were being pursued by their oppressors. But if we didn't wish to be dependent on the natives, there were at least fifty uninhabited islands. Who would ever find us in this maze of a hundred and fifty islands, with the Malay archipelago near by? But on the other hand, why escape? We shouldn't even be considering flight. We mustn't add to our original mistake. Flight would be a first step in our believing in the crime ourselves. No. It had to stop right here. We must go back to Tahiti, and with the *Niuroahiti*, for without her, we would be arrested immediately. Then, Mirey, furious at seeing his blackmail scheme go up in smoke, would be all the more eager to denounce us, what with his lust for revenge, not to mention money. Now that he had shown his true colors, staying around would be very dangerous for us. That's when we finally understood the extent of our terrible blunder at not returning to Tahiti immediately after the crew's desertion.

"It would be easy enough to escape in the whaleboat. But then we would have to give up thinking about Tahiti. But if we went into hiding, it would be a tacit admission that we had done something wrong. We would be living like outlaws! Worst of all, it would inflict great harm on the schooner's owner, for the Spaniards would not be likely to relinquish the prize our stupidity had delivered into their hands. So, stay we must, since after all our consciences were clear.

"There was only one thing that really troubled us, and that was our papers. I've already said that the *Niuroahiti*'s papers were not on board. We therefore had to try to get by with fictitious papers. We also had hopes that once Mirey had slept off his drunken binge, he wouldn't dare stick with the story he had told the day before. Even if he were punished for his bad behavior and evil intentions, we didn't think he'd go so far as to accuse two men of something that might cost them their lives.

"My brother suggested he go see the governor the next day and arrange things amicably. I would leave for Tahiti the same day.

"At five in the morning, we were awakened by a big noise on deck. I climbed up, but I'd no sooner cleared the companion hatch than a Spanish officer thrust his bayonet at my chest and shouted 'Alto!' Two launches full of armed sailors were tied up alongside the ship. Thirty naval infantrymen were on the deck, armed to the teeth. Brushing aside the officer's bayonet and his 'Alto,' I leapt back into the cabin. Something told me: 'Don't give yourself up; you'll live to regret it.' So I called out: 'Alexander, the Spaniards are here. They've come to arrest us,' I picked up my Winchester rifle and Alexander did the same.

"What should we do? Fight these dogs? We wouldn't last five minutes. We could blow each other's brains out. But what would people say? That we were two pirates who, seeing we were caught, got ourselves killed, or killed each other? No, that was out of the question.

"The men who had deserted to Tetiaroa would have found a boat—or built one—by now, and would have arrived at Tahiti or Moorea across from Papeete. Where else could they have gone, unless they went all the way to Samoa? In any case, we'd find them and they'd show Mirey up for the liar he was.

"So, we gave ourselves up."

VII

WHILE JOSEPH'S DEPOSITION, elaborated during the long months of detention, contained some accurate statements about authenticated happenings, it was also full of assertions as extravagant as they were untrue. And what gave strength to the lies was the degree of truth they contained.

When Joseph was describing life on board the schooner, or a character like Tehahe, his sense of realistic detail was admirable. There was many a captain like Tehahe around Tahiti: Tianoa, for instance, when he was aboard ship on a Sunday, celebrated Mass in an old frock coat that had once belonged to a missionary priest. And if he happened to miss an island—which was not infrequent—he would bury himself in his Bible to find a verse that might direct him back on course.

Helmsmen who fell asleep at the wheel after a day of exhausting work were no rarity either, as the many shipwrecks on the atolls attested. Nor was it unusual for hardened sailors like the Roriques to awaken the offender by smacking him in the face with a swab.

And again, Joseph aptly described the state of mind

that developed and the incidents that occurred on a small ship where the captain held only the vaguest local certificate seconded by a master mariner. But when Joseph wrote that Tehahe threatened Alexander with a revolver, he taxes one's credulity. Not to this day has a Tahitian captain ever had firearms on board ship. This is precisely what made navigation different in the archipelagos of eastern Polynesia from Melanesia, where the traders' ships were heavily armed. The incident involving Tehahe and the revolver was laughed at by all sailors familiar with Tahiti.

The story of the sailors jumping into the sea when the schooner approached the atoll of Tetiaroa was equally unbelievable. Tetiaroa (which today belongs to the actor Marlon Brando) was, as has been told, an atoll thirty miles from Tahiti owned by Prince Hinoi Pomare, also owner of the *Niuroahiti*. His men went there from time to time to collect coconuts and make copra, which they shipped out on a small schooner at fairly regular intervals. To load the schooner, they used a whaleboat which, when not in use, was pulled ashore and left in a shelter made of coconut leaves to protect it from the sun. If we are to believe the Roriques, this whaleboat was to take the deserting sailors to Papeete ahead of the *Niuroahiti*, thus enabling them to give their version of the events first. It is hard to believe that the captain of a well-rigged schooner sailing straight for Tahiti with a following wind would have anything to fear from a heavy, squat boat powered by oars. But since the men were never seen again, and the whaleboat was found in its proper place on the island and not abandoned somewhere along the Tahitian coast, it becomes evident that the men never set foot on Tetiaroa.

And what of Mirey, a dull-witted native whom Joseph presents as the diabolical advisor naively listened to by the two adventurers—a farcical character dropped into the middle of a tragedy?

At this juncture, the results of the inquiries made by the French consuls in Durban and Capetown finally reached the judiciary in Brest. And very disappointing they were. Neither in the Transvaal nor in the province of the Cape had anyone been able to identify the Roriques. Crespin was both infuriated and devastated by the news. The brothers, on the other hand, were jubilant: "They must have done a pretty poor job of research. We continue to stand by what we said."

Three months of investigation had produced virtually no results. The Vice-Admiral was only too well aware of the fact and, goaded by journalists from Paris who kept asking when the brothers would be brought to trial, he relieved Crespin of his functions and advised him to exercise his rights to retirement. He was replaced by Maupin, also a frigate commander, who had to begin the investigation all over again.

The Roriques made no attempt to hide their satisfaction at this turn of events, for they still held a trump card: the fact that their identity was impossible to verify. For all that it had exceptional jurisdiction, the Naval Tribunal was hardly an emergency court-martial: it had to respect certain procedures.

Maupin, a shrewder man than Crespin, did not labor under his predecessor's preconceived ideas. Changing the venue of the interrogation, he had the brothers transferred to the Naval Tribunal on the left bank of the Penfeld, outside the walls of the naval port. For the time being, this won him the prisoners' gratitude. The trip took about twenty minutes, and although each was handcuffed to a policeman, they were grateful for the walk after their long hours in their cells. They had to cross the Penfeld by the Pont Trehouart, the swing bridge that opened to let boats through. While they waited, the sailors and workmen in the arsenal stared at them, but without hostility or even disapproval.

Since the prison of Pontaniou and the Tribunal were on opposite sides of the Penfeld beyond the port walls, the brothers had to walk a considerable distance, first down the Grand'Rue, then through the faubourg of Recouvrance. It was on one of these journeys that a curious incident took place. A woman was doing her wash in the public laundry. She stood up as the brothers walked past, and suddenly a look of astonishment crossed her face. She was about to say something when Joseph, who had also noticed her, raised his manacled hands in a gesture of warning. Riveted to the spot, the poor woman stood in stunned silence.

The Naval Tribunal was housed in a dark building dating back to the seventeenth century, part of which arched over the narrow street, named for that reason the rue de la Voute. It was a sinister place, especially at night, when a solitary street light made a pale circle on the cobblestones.

It was here, in this dimly lighted room with its moldy mahogany paneling that several dramas of the high seas saw their final acts played out. One of the most celebrated, and still well remembered, was the case of the *Foederis Arca* that caused four heads to fall.

Article 4 of the Law of April 10, 1825, states that mutineers sentenced to death shall be shot, but that pirates must be beheaded. Now, the Roriques were charged with two crimes, that of piracy and murder, each one carrying the death penalty. The act of taking possession of a ship, even where no murder was committed, constituted the crime of piracy as defined by this law.

Maupin, in an attempt to determine their identities, tried to learn something of their lives before they had arrived in Rarotonga. The two brothers had mentioned sailing on several ships, in California, Australia and elsewhere. But how were these assertions to be verified at a time when mails were slow and telegraphic communications few and precarious? They maintained that, having always been properly registered, corroboration could be found by getting in touch with the captain of any of the ships on which they had sailed—for example, the *Vagabond* from Sydney, which had originally dropped them at Penrhyn.

Maupin was not eager to engage in the task of finding, somewhere in the vast Pacific, a three-masted schooner practicing "tramping," and whose name might well be pure fantasy. However, he did file a request for an investigation which, passing through a series of offices and up the ladder of various administrative bureaus, ended up with the British authorities, and finally the Australians.

The British have the reputation of being a methodical and persevering people. It was proved conclusively in this case, for they not only found the *Vagabond*, but also its logbook, which was eventually delivered to the Tribunal in Brest. The document was accompanied by a note from the British Embassy, with the tongue-in-cheek observation: "After reading the logbook, it is hard to understand why the accused were so determined to find it, unless they thought its recovery to be virtually impossible."

The logbook read as follows:

"August 4, 1890: Alexander and Joseph Rorique refuse to wash the deck when ordered to do so by the captain.

"August 5, 1890: These men mistreat and insult the mate. Through their influence on the other men, the Roriques have brought work on board to a standstill, and they themselves do as little work as possible.

"August 21, 1890: Mr. Campbell tells me that Alexander Rorique refuses to take soundings when ordered to do so.

"September 10: Suspected of stealing.

"September 16: The captain, the first and second petty officers, the cook and the carpenter were suddenly taken ill after eating beef. Violent intestinal pains and vomiting resulted. Suspect they were poisoned. The illness lasted twenty-four hours.

"September 21: Joseph Rorique struck the cook.

"September 22: The captain was told that the cook saw Joseph Rorique destroy certain objects and instruments, but he didn't dare say anything for fear the two brothers would beat him to death.

"October 6: Joseph Rorique is threatened with reprisal for refusing to obey. His and his brother's behavior is very bad and has an evil influence on the other men.

"October 18: Alexander refuses to obey the second petty officer.

"October 19: Joseph tried to kill the cook but was prevented by members of the crew. This man and his brother cause great trouble on board. The captain and first petty officer are armed at all times and always on their guard. They are afraid that these malefactors will try to bring about a shipwreck. They have asked to leave the ship but the captain has told them he won't do it until they reach Sydney.

"February 6, 1891: Moored in Penrhyn. Alexander and Joseph Rorique deserted during the night, taking their belongings with them."

This concise journal gives eloquent testimony to the fact that under the friendly, polite, almost refined veneer they showed in society, the brothers had violent and cynical natures.

In addition, Maupin had good reason to believe that Joseph's incriminating letter to Alexander when the latter was in Kaukura indicated clear evidence of premeditation. Since Maupin assumed Joseph had forgotten its existence, he counted on the Roriques' surprise at the revelation of this important piece of evidence, and how it would shatter their confidence.

But he didn't know the Roriques. Joseph and Alexander had long ago devised a plan of action in case the compromising letter turned up. They weren't so naive as to think that, having failed to reach its destination, it would disappear into the void for all time. So, when Maupin, after cleverly setting the stage, presented the damning letter, all he got for his pains were condescending smiles and the painful discovery that he was the loser in the battle of wits.

Of course Joseph remembered the letter, but the schooner in question wasn't the *Henry*, and even less the *Niuroahiti*—which he hadn't even known at that point: it concerned a ship out of commission in Papeete belonging to Coppenrath, which they had considered buying.

Was it their fault if the letter was written in a Flemish-Dutch dialect they had spoken since they were children and still used in South Africa, where it had been brought by Dutch emigrants? Besides, the French translation was very bad and they demanded a retranslation.

Thus Maupin was a long way from the triumph he had hoped for.

As the time allotted for the interrogation began to run out, it became all too clear that its results were far from impressive. In reconstituting the drama, Maupin had tried to understand the role each of the actors had played. Mirey's was particularly unclear. In the main, he had un-doubtedly told the truth, but was he hiding anything? Why had he been spared? The pirates had no reason to preserve this dangerous witness; to help sail the ship, an Atiu sailor would have been far preferable, and besides, speaking neither French nor English, he wouldn't have been able to communicate with foreigners. So it seemed obvious that the Roriques thought Mirey sufficiently com-promised not to inform on them.

The poisoning of the two sailors on the *Niuroahiti* with rum, and the extreme indisposition of the people on the *Vagabond* led Maupin to seek the advice of the chief navy pharmacist for the port of Brest. On reading Mirey's description of the victim's symptoms, he deduced that they had been poisoned by arsenic, a white, stable, odorless and tasteless powder that mixes well with any kind of food but is almost insoluble in water or spirits.

In a bottle of rum, arsenic would have made a white precipitate that would naturally have attracted attention. It therefore made more sense to put the poison in food, and who better than the cook?

Going back to Mirey's deposition: When he threw himself at the brothers' feet and begged them for mercy, it may have occurred to them to put Mirey to the test by giving him the poison to kill the rest of the crew. Tehahe and Gibson had been dispatched quickly enough, but it was not likely that the four sailors would let themselves be shot, one after the other. Even without firearms, barricaded in the forward quarters they could be dangerous just by acting in concert. Therefore, the poison of which they knew nothing became the ideal instrument. And Mirey, in order to lessen his responsibility, may have invented the story of the rum and the sailors driven at gun point to jump into the sea. This in no way reduced the Roriques' guilt, but it mitigated Mirey's if it could be proven that he had acted under pain of death.

Maupin began to realize that the case, seemingly simple at the outset, was not so easy to present to a court where it threatened to arouse powerful emotions. It was based on the deposition of a single witness, himself indicted, and two accused men about whom nobody knew anything, but for whom the public showed considerable sympathy. These were elements that a clever defense lawyer could exploit to the detriment of the prosecution. Should one

lie turn up in Mirey's deposition, the whole patiently con-
structed edifice would come tumbling down.

The Vice-Admiral was visibly upset by the interest the
public and press showed in the case. He therefore issued
orders that everything, including the trial, be terminated
by December 31. Pressed for time, Maupin had no alterna-
tive but to consider the investigation closed; he filed his
report on November 17.

So far as the crime of piracy was concerned—as defined
in Article 4 of the Law of April 10, 1825—the judge advo-
cate was of the opinion that this was well enough estab-
lished just by the fact that when Alexander arrived in
Ponape, he told the Spanish authorities that he was "the
sole owner and captain of the ship." The case for the
murders, however, rested exclusively on Mirey's allegations.

The report concluded: "Even though Alexander Rorique played the principal role in the drama of the *Niuroahiti*, the law of April 10, 1825, was directed solely at
those individuals who made up the crew. Since this man
was only a passenger, he can be accused only of complicity.
It is therefore my judgment that there are enough charges
to bring Joseph Rorique to trial before the First Naval
Tribunal in Brest, as a member of the crew of the French
schooner *Niuroahiti*, accused of the crime of piracy to
which must be added the aggravating circumstance that
the crime was preceded, accompanied, and followed by
homicide."

Thus Alexander, who had been considered the most
guilty, and Mirey, the lone witness, were each charged
only with complicity—a curious paradox indeed.

The Naval Tribunal was drawn by lot and included the following:

Compristo: Ship's captain, the President
Le Gall la Salle: Judge of the Civil Tribunal in Brest
Manceau: Judge of the Civil Tribunal in Brest
Goubet: Navy Purser
Caill: Ship's Lieutenant
de Kerros: Ship's Lieutenant
Rousseau: Assistant Naval Engineer
To which must be added: *Maupin,* Frigate Captain,
and government commissioner
Ribouillet: Naval Infantry Captain and Clerk

The last two had no voice in the proceedings.

As luck would have it, Compristo was a fat, red-faced, grotesque man nicknamed Medaille. It was said that his ancestor—a gendarme—captured a famous Corsican bandit by the name of Compristo, and for this valorous deed, he received a decoration which earned him the name "Medaille." When a confused journalist, thinking he was doing the correct thing, addressed him as "Medaille de Compristo," he was told: "Just call me Compristo. I gave up the gendarme's name for the bandit's."

In September, the Roriques had written Maîtres Demange and Laguerre, two well-known lawyers of the Paris bar, asking them to take on their defense. They never received an answer, and Joseph later accused Maupin of intercepting the letter. On December 1, they were told that they had three days in which to find a lawyer. When Maître de Chamaillard from the Rennes bar, assisted by Maître Dubois from Brest, offered their services, and for nothing, the brothers accepted gratefully. However, in the little time remaining—it was the last day of the hearings—Chamaillard had only eight hours in which to consult the files and take notes. On visiting the accused, he suggested to Joseph that he take on his defense and that Maître Dubois take on Alexander's. He made no attempt to hide the fact that, owing to certain contradictions in Mirey's deposition, his case would be easier to defend than Alexander's. But Joseph was adamant: "You either defend us both or you don't defend us at all. We've been through too much together to have our cases separated at the last moment. Also, let me warn you that if you say one word that could exonerate me to the detriment of my brother, I shall stop you and protest to the Tribunal."

Although the lawyer was full of admiration for this show of brotherly devotion, he made it clear that under these conditions, the trial was bound to go against both of them equally.

On December 5, 1893, the solemn proceedings got under way. The weather was dreary, and the early morning drizzle grew gradually heavier, coating robes and uniforms with glistening droplets. A crowd had gathered around the entrance to the Tribunal, and the guards, bayonets in their rifles, presented arms as the court made its entrance —the officers in full dress with swords and epaulets, the civil judges in robes, mortars and ermine-tipped cloaks.

In the midst of all this decorum, the accused held their own. They were dressed in respectable civilian clothes, beards and mustaches carefully trimmed. With their dignified bearing and look of confidence, they appeared little affected by the ceremonial.

Mirey, lost in an overcoat much too large for him, looked even more the frightened weasel than usual. And for all the gravity of the place and moment, the poor natives from the Gilbert Islands—Baku and Korotu—were cause for hilarity. Since their regular sailors' clothes were considered unsuitable for the occasion, the Sisters at the Naval Hospital had been pressed into service to devise some sort of civilian dress. The results were masterpieces of artlessness and bad workmanship.

The courtroom was too small for the crowd, so a large part of it had to remain outside. There were many seamen in the audience, and also a number of journalists from Brest, Rennes, Nantes and even Paris, especially from the newspaper *Les Débats*. The trial, recalling the heady days of the buccaneers, had excited the curiosity of the entire nation.

From the outset, the examination foundered on the question of the Roriques' identity. For all the President's earnest prodding, they persisted in claiming that their names were Joseph and Alexander Rorique, born in Port Natal and Pretoria respectively, where all attempts at tracing them had proved fruitless.

At this point, some unexpected evidence came into the Tribunal's hands. It appeared that a Norwegian sailor named Albert Blom Bore, landing in Tahiti from the packet boat *City of Papeete*, reported seeing Joseph on the *Niuroahiti*'s deck and thought he recognized him as a childhood friend by the name of Henri Oftebro from Stavanger, who had a brother Sved and whose father was a missionary priest in Zululand.

When he was questioned on the matter, Joseph said

with disdain: "I don't know the gentleman, and I am not the son of a priest." When the judiciary looked into the matter, the real Oftebro brothers turned up in the Transvaal.

Compristo was beginning to have his hands full with these insolent young men who refused to be intimidated, had an answer for everything, and zealously declared that they could prove their innocence. They defended themselves at every step of the way, sticking to their version of the story, denying any other, even including sometimes the evidence.

The President, for whom calm and patience were not outstanding attributes, became increasingly excitable. He was not used to this kind of debate, and little by little, the examination turned into an indictment, as the defense was quick to point out. Chamaillard's protestations were polite but firm, and Compristo, made circumspect by the presence of so many journalists, had to watch his step.

The events as described by the accused focused the audience's attention on the first scene of the drama: the one in which Captain Tehahe threatened, then tried unsuccessfully to fire at Alexander. How could the captain of a Tahitian schooner come by a revolver and ammunition in a country without a single gunsmith's shop? And besides, why would he have bought one? Certainly not in order to protect himself against a Polynesian crew who were his own countrymen, and where, if they had had differences, they would have limited themselves to fisticuffs.

In the heat of the discussion, Alexander remembered having given the gun to Tehahe because "he liked to shoot at sea birds."

"So," the President replied, "you not only taught Te-hahe your bad habits, but sold him one of your revolvers so that he could aim it at you!"

On the other hand, a discussion about Gibson's death and how he was thrown into the sea by a swinging main-sail boom went against Compristo.

"This accident," he said peremptorily, "could happen only if you're coming about in a following wind; in a head wind, it's inconceivable."

Alexander's explanation was entirely plausible: "As the *Niuroahiti* was on a starboard tack and with no one at the helm because of the mutiny, the ship gradually came into the wind. At that moment, the mainsail, held to port by the tiller, carried the ship into a head wind and a port tack. In coming about, the sail was put under such a strain that the boom tackle gave way. The suddenly freed boom swept violently to starboard, knocking Gibson, who was standing on the deckhouse, right into the sea."

Whether or not this version was true, it was certainly reasonable. But Compristo was not impressed:

"You've invented the entire story. All fore-and-aft main-sails have two sheets to prevent this kind of accident."

"Perhaps on navy ships," Alexander replied, "where there is enough crew to haul in or ease off one sheet, then the other, but you can't do that on a commercial schooner. We have to settle for a boom tackle made fast to the side opposite the wind."

From this, it appeared that the President wasn't too familiar with the rigging on American-made schooners plying the Pacific. But his sailor's pride—at a time when the navy still counted several sailing ships among its vessels—made him determined to have the last word.

And so the debate wandered off the subject and, to Maupin's despair, completely lost sight of its main objective.

Interestingly enough, two days after the Roriques' trial, a British schooner coming into the port of Brest had the very same accident. A man was thrown into the sea, picked up and taken to the naval hospital, where he died. Impressed by the coincidence, a doctor wrote an article for a Paris newspaper entitled: "The Finger of God."

With lofty sarcasm, Alexander refuted the President's implication that he and his brother had been planning the affair over a long period:

"We have been accused of purchasing a logbook and sextant. This fact apparently proves that we had decided to leave the French possessions in the South Pacific. You cite as proof that owners of local schooners relied solely on navigation by dead reckoning, without the aid of instruments. I don't see how the Navy can criticize us for wanting to use scientific means for sailing among the Tuamotus—famous as a dangerous archipelago and for good reason—when the Navy itself, at the very time we were there in July 1891, lost the cutter *Volage* on an atoll in full daylight."

Alexander was making little effort to endear himself to the Tribunal and its majority of naval officers. During the course of the interrogation, the Roriques had insisted that a model be made of the *Niuroahiti*, or more exactly, a small-scale model of the ship's deck, which would have

[135]

been a simple matter in a port like Brest. They maintained, with some justice, that as the different scenes of the drama had taken place on a stage no larger than a few square yards, it behooved the Tribunal to know exactly how the ship was designed and the location of each of the actors.

Today, it would not be necessary for the accused to make such a request. The magistrate charged with reconstituting the crime would, in the event he could not do it on the ship itself, be forced to re-create it in some other way. Even then, it was surprising to have Maupin refuse to comply with a request that would have helped clarify many questions.

Specifically, the brothers claimed that it was impossible for Mirey, who was in the large cabin, to see Alexander at the cathead, and even more, to be able to hear him talking to the men on the bowsprit. And furthermore, Mirey testified that Tehahe fell on sacks of mother-of-pearl behind the helm, where it was manifestly impossible to stow anything, especially such a heavy load.

How, without a plan or model, could the truth of these assertions be verified? And why was Maupin so obstinate about resisting the suggestion? The only possible explanation is that, since the indictment was based entirely on Mirey's deposition, he feared that certain contradictions might come to light. Being convinced of the Roriques' guilt in the murder of Tehahe and Gibson, and determined that they receive capital punishment, he thought it beside the point to find out if the rest of the crew was killed by them or by somebody else.

The prosecution summoned two witnesses from Tahiti.

The first, Goupil, Gibson's brother-in-law, represented the plaintiff in the person of Gibson's widow. He produced the now familiar copy of the *Messager de Tahiti* with the headline "Horrible Tragedy—Sextuple Assassination, etc.," as well as a letter from Gibson's widow demanding suitable punishment for her husband's murderers. Compristo read the letter out loud, against the protestations of the defense, which felt the President was taking too many procedural liberties.

The other witness from Tahiti was André, pilot of the *Henry*, whom Joseph had served. (It is worth noting that neither of the two witnesses knew any more about the case than had already come out.) André's deposition was very damaging to Joseph. He maintained that he had always been suspicious of him and that he watched him day and night. When Joseph insisted that the ship take him to Kaukura, where his brother was, André became convinced that he was up to something. Moreover, if anyone had listened to him and done as he suggested, Joseph Rorique would have been put out of harm's way in Papeete, before he ever set foot on the *Niuroahiti*. The defense promptly noted that although he had sworn to "testify without prejudice," André's present attitude seemed at variance with the one he demonstrated when, moored at Anaa, he left Joseph in sole command of the ship for five days, and that moreover, he had invited him to dinner at his house in Papeete the very evening before Joseph's departure.

Both the audience and Tribunal were somewhat taken aback by André's deposition and wondered at the reason for his present hostility. When the trial was over, the editor of *Le Petit Quotidien* wrote: "André, the pilot, was noticeably exuberant between sessions of the trial. On one occasion, he was heard to say: 'This is all a waste of time. Too many formalities. The Roriques should have their heads chopped off without further ado. They deserve it a hundred times over.' Coming from a witness's lips, these words indicated a certain ill will, to say the least."

During Mirey's account of the events, the defense asked the President for the names of the two sailors who were supposed to have climbed under the bowsprit and jumped into the sea to avoid Alexander's gun. "Farina and Pitau," Mirey replied. The two brothers jumped up and asked to be heard in one voice. At first, Compristo was furious and threatened to have them removed from the court-room and to continue the trial without them. Then, struck by the spontaneity of their response, he decided to let Alexander speak.

"He lies! That man lies, and I can prove it!" he shouted. "One of the men he says climbed under the bowsprit couldn't possibly have done it because he had a game foot. I don't know if Pitau had a clubfoot or had had some sort of accident, but even though he was an excellent sailor, he couldn't have climbed the rigging or made the kind of maneuver we've been describing." Alexander's eyes glistened and his lips curled with a smile of triumph.

The audience was impressed and several people stood up. Maître de Chamaillard's satisfaction was manifest, while Compristo looked confused. Hesitating for a moment, he noticed that André, his deposition finished, had taken a seat in the audience. He called him back into the dock and without bothering to swear him in again, asked:

"As a pilot in a small port like Papeete, you must have known practically all the sailors on the local ships. Did you know Pitau?"

"Yes, I did."

"Did he have a game foot as has been claimed?"

There was a pregnant silence.

"I . . . I don't think so."

"He doesn't dare tell a complete lie," Alexander muttered in a rage, within earshot of the guards.

The President turned toward the accused: "This incident was staged entirely by you."

Crestfallen, the audience settled back as the brothers' faces turned ashen.

Was it a blunder on André's part or a deliberate act? His state of mind during his deposition was hard to fathom. But the public's attitude proved significant. Fifteen years later, on August 14, 1909, when André had retired to the island of Noirmoutier, he sent the Minister of the Navy this curious letter:

"As the result of a sermon delivered by the local priest, M. Boisseau, on November 19, 1908, in the church of La Guerinière at Noirmoutier, I filed suit for defamation. M. Abbé Boisseau accused me of bearing false witness, thereby causing the conviction of the Rorique brothers for acts of piracy before the Naval Tribunal in Brest where I had been summoned as a witness . . ."

Eight sessions of the Tribunal were scheduled from December 5 to 8, 1893. The courtroom was crowded throughout, and on the last day, a mob filled the narrow rue de la Voute.

The government prosecutor based his indictment on the fact that premeditation was proved by Joseph's letter to his brother: "Even if we had not had Mirey's deposition, even if he too had disappeared in this incident, the letter alone would be enough to indict the Roriques."

The brothers' defense on this point was not very convincing. It consisted of arguments about certain words and expressions that belonged to another dialect—for there were several, they said—and to assert that the retranslation they had asked for had not been granted, which was true. But it was also likely that had a retranslation been made, it would probably have modified only a few details, leaving the basic facts unchanged—in other words, damaging to the accused.

Maupin went further: "Up to this day, in most cases of piracy, alcohol has always played an important role. Here, we have something quite different. The accused are professional pirates, just as other men are doctors or lawyers. They made and executed their plans with a total lack of moral sense, removing all possibility of clemency. If a criminal's responsibility is proportionate to his intellectual capacity, then the Roriques' responsibility is total, for they have demonstrated very exceptional faculties. For all these reasons, I recommend that the Tribunal show no pity."

When it came time for the rebuttal, the tension in the room was at fever pitch. Chamaillard's was awaited with special anticipation, for he was known for his defense of some particularly challenging cases before the Tribunals in Rennes and Quimper.

He had little trouble showing up the weaknesses of an

indictment that rested solely on the testimony of a more or less tainted individual. He reminded his listeners of a case a few years earlier in which one de Segonzac, an officer in the African army, was accused of murdering his comrade, Quinquerez, by a cadre of five soldiers wearing the French uniform, and was acquitted.

"With this as an example," he said, "how can you convict two men on the testimony of an habitual criminal who admits to being inside the cabin when the incidents were taking place on deck?"

Chamaillard went on to note that certain dramas of the sea had involved even more unusual disappearances than those on the *Niuroahiti*. Take the case of the *Marie Celeste*, a brig sailing from New York on November 7, 1872, with a crew of five, two officers and its captain, Benjamin Brigg, and his wife and child. On December 6, the ship was sighted by the brig *Dei Gracia* near Santa Maria in the Azores, heading under full sail in a southeasterly direction. As the ship was well known to Moorhouse, the *Dei Gracia*'s captain, its strange behavior caused him to approach it to within shouting distance. To his astonishment, he saw that there was no one at the helm, nor anyone on deck. Three men rowed over in a dinghy and reported that it had neither crew nor passengers. The *Marie Celeste* was a deserted ship. Yet the schooner was in good condition, with no sign of struggle or violence of any kind. And there was fresh, uneaten food on the table. "After twenty years, this drama remains as inexplicable as it was on the very first day.

"Are we then to believe that if by some miracle a survivor had been found, the law's first task was to suspect

[141]

him of murdering his companions and thus require him to prove his innocence?"

With passionate eloquence, Chamaillard continued his rebuttal, insisting that if a shred of doubt existed—which was indeed the case here—he must move in favor of the accused.

A pale winter sun cast a few faint rays on the mahogany paneling. Then, gradually, darkness filled the lugubrious room, lit by a few gas lamps that bathed the audience in a greenish glow.

At this very moment, on the other side of the world, a radiant morning was dawning over the Tuamotu archipelago. The *maoae*, the trade winds out of the northeast, were blowing hard, whipping up whitecaps on the intense blue of the sea and shaking the tops of the tall coconut trees, their stems waving with an almost feminine grace. In the lagoons, the colors varied according to depth, from emerald to turquoise to amethyst, ending as topaz reflections at the edge of the sea.

Perhaps the memory of such a morning flitted through the minds of those in the courtroom who had known the Pacific, their spirits for a moment taking flight from the dark rainy city, far from this gray crowd that smelled like wet dogs.

A distant noise like that of a flock of sheep on the move penetrated the courtroom, growing louder and louder. Hundreds of wooden shoes—*socques*, they called them in Brest—hammered against the wet pavement. The workmen in the navy yard were done for the day.

The hearings were over. The accused left the courtroom and the Tribunal retired for its deliberations.

They were asked seven questions. The first two involved the act of piracy as committed by Alexander and Joseph Rorique; the Tribunal was unanimously in the affirmative. The third question concerned Mirey's guilt; the answer was a unanimous "no." The fourth involved Tehahe's murder; the fifth, Gibson's. To these two questions, six voted "yes" and one "no." At least one member of the Tribunal could not with a clear conscience sentence two men to death on the strength of Mirey's testimony.

As for the passenger's death, there were two affirmative and five negative votes. And finally, on the subject of the two poisoned sailors, there were six "yes" and one "no." Of the sailors who threw themselves into the sea under the threat of Alexander's gun, the government prosecutor preferred not to pose the question.

"Accordingly, the Tribunal condemns Alexander and Joseph Rorique to death, and specifies that their execution take place in Brest, where they will be beheaded." Mirey was acquitted.

The accused were brought back into the now empty courtroom and the Tribunal dismissed, with only guards at shoulder arms to hear the government prosecutor pronounce the sentence. Maupin read Joseph's first, then Alexander's—who appeared more deeply affected by his brother's sentence than by his own. Some had thought it possible that Joseph's would be limited to hard labor for life. The two brothers embraced, and Joseph murmured: "Come on, be brave. Don't let them see you're crying; they'll think they've frightened you."

As the police were taking the two men away, Maupin said: "Don't think this is the end of the matter. The last word hasn't been spoken yet." What could the prosecutor have meant by this strange statement?

Outside, the crowd filled the street all the way to the Grand'Rue. Some of the women were visibly moved as the condemned men passed by. Whatever their crimes might have been, they were almost forgotten, the passage of time and distance from the site having mitigated their seriousness. One old Breton woman, seeing them go by, cried out: "You poor boys!" threw her apron over her face and burst into sobs.

Alexander and Joseph were given a compassionate welcome by Compredon, the warden at the prison Pontaniou, and he allowed them to stay together a few hours. Two days later, their lawyers had the Roriques sign a petition for their pardon, addressed to Sadi Carnot, President of the French Republic. Then, under the shadow of the guillotine, the anguished wait began.

VIII

DURING THE MONTH of January 1894, a Belgian steamship, captained by a German named Schmidt, came into Brest because it had been damaged in a storm off the island of Ouessant.

People were still talking about the Roriques, and the pilot who came on board told the captain about the trial, and the fact that he himself had been in the audience at the Naval Tribunal. He gave an exact description of the accused, mentioning their age, appearance and a few telling details. Suddenly Schmidt exclaimed: "I know those two men—two brothers who answer your description exactly! But their name wasn't Rorique; they had a very French name . . . it begins with a 'de' . . . Degrave! That's it!"

His curiosity whetted, the pilot found an old issue of the *Dépêche de Brest*, and showed Schmidt the brothers' photographs. This time, the captain was categorical: They were indeed the Degrave brothers whom he'd known during the course of his voyages.

The very next morning, the front page of the *Dépêche*

de Brest carried the bold headline: GERMAN REVEALS REAL IDENTITY OF RORIQUE BROTHERS.

The news created a sensation, but there was more to come: Two days later, the naval court revealed that some time ago, it had received an anonymous letter that said: "The Rorique brothers were not born in the Transvaal. They are natives of Ostend, Belgium, and their names are Léonce Degrave and his younger brother Eugène. They left Antwerp almost four years ago on a British ship sailing to Australia. They pretended to be natives of the Transvaal because Dutch is spoken there, and they were afraid they might give themselves away when they spoke Flemish or the dialect of Ostend, which resembles Dutch. It is therefore hardly surprising that no one was able to find information or certificates of birth in Pretoria or Port Natal. You can, on the other hand, obtain full information about them from the Mayor of Ostend."

This letter, written on a page torn from a notebook, reached the Tribunal on December 10, two days after the end of the trial. At least, that is what was penciled in on the margin. Why did the author wait for the brothers' conviction before revealing their identities? Some cynics wondered if the letter hadn't arrived during the trial, which might explain Maupin's oracular words after the reading of the verdict. In that case, Captain Schmidt—without realizing it—rendered French justice a singular service by preventing it from beheading two convicts under false names. From then on, information about the Degraves—alias Roriques—began to pour into the offices of the naval judiciary.

Léonce Degrave, born at Ostend on May 10, 1854, was

the son of Jacques Tilleman Degrave and Clementine de Bruyne. Eugène was also born at Ostend, on March 4, 1865. They belonged to one of the best families in Belgium. A third brother, Auguste, was a stockbroker in Antwerp, and a sister still lived with their mother in Ostend.

How could the interrogation, with this information at its disposal, wander so far afield without discovering the brothers' identities? Here were two brothers, excellent mariners, speaking perfect French, as well as a dialect spoken on the Belgian-Dutch frontier, and Narrhum had stated in Ponape that they themselves said they were Belgian!

The issue of the *Messager de Tahiti* with this particular detail had even been circulated among the members of the Tribunal during the hearings. But it failed to change the course of the magistrate's inquiries. Nor was Crespin's attention diverted for so much as a moment, so convinced was he that the accused were escaped convicts. Maupin showed hardly more perspicacity, but he did receive on December 10 a letter from one Le Bon of 10 rue de Flandres in Ostend confirming all the facts revealed in the anonymous letter. This one therefore could not have been received on that date, and the "December 10" written in its margin, in what must have been Maupin's own hand, could only refer to the date on which the information was corroborated by Le Bon's letter.

All the evidence would indicate that Maupin knew of these revelations at least during the trial, if not before. Why was this letter not included immediately in the dossier? Perhaps Maupin was not wholly responsible. The

Port Admiral for the Second Region—who in some areas represented the prosecutor in this special jurisdiction—had stated that everything must be concluded by December 31. In his view, as in Crespin's, the case was very simple: these men were criminals condemned by a legally constituted Tribunal. So it mattered little if they were executed under one name or another; the verification could come later. This, among many other things, is precisely what the Naval Tribunal was reproached for later.

Meanwhile, as information about the Degraves flooded Brest, their past was gradually pieced together. And what a past! Extraordinary is too mild a word for it.

Now convicted murderers, these two men had risked their lives to save a total of thirty men under a variety of circumstances—and with no thought of remuneration. The accumulating evidence revealed the following:

"Léonce Degrave finished his military service with the 7th Belgian line-infantry, and was promoted to junior officer for having, on January 30, 1871, in very cold weather and in total darkness, placed his own life in peril to save a soldier who had fallen into the canal of l'Espierre. He was decorated with a silver medal by royal order in September 1871.

"In 1874, the city of Liège bestowed another silver medal on him when he again risked his life to save that of a drowning man.

"Léonce Degrave left the army before the end of his term of service by virtue of an honorable discharge granted him in return for acts of courage and devotion, and he entered the service of the State as a pilot-in-training in the port of Antwerp.

"During his stay in this city, he rescued a sailor from the British steamship *Knight Templar* who had fallen into the harbor, and he was awarded a rescue medal by royal order on September 8, 1883.

"In 1882, he passed the exams for lieutenant in foreign trade, and in that capacity, sailed that same year on the *Euclid*, in 1883 on the *Carvilair*, in 1884 on the *Wilhelm and Albert*, and the *Castel Pak*. He even obtained command of a small British steamship, on which his brother Joseph was first mate.

"At the start of 1885, using all the money at their disposal, a part of which was loaned by their mother, they had a steam trawler built named the *Degrave*, which they used for fishing, with a crew of four sailors recruited in Ostend.

"On October 24, finding themselves in very heavy weather in the North Sea near Doggerbank, they sighted a three-masted Norwegian schooner, the *Pieter*, in distress. The mizzen and mainsail were torn right down to the deck and as the sails fell, their gaffs had crushed the lifeboats secured in the fore and aft passages. The crew had sought refuge in the forecastle and were making desperate signs to be rescued. As none of the men on the *Degrave* were willing to put out in a rowboat on a raging sea, Léonce and Eugène decided to do so alone. It took them four trips to bring the twelve men from the *Pieter* to the *Degrave*. Léonce crushed three fingers of his right hand while trying to hold the boat alongside the *Degrave* so that his brother could get the captain on board whom he had found sick in his bunk. The *Pieter* sank soon after, and as the bad weather prevented their return to

[149]

Ostend, the *Degrave* dropped the men off at Scarborough on the English coast.

"Two weeks later, on November 6, the *Degrave* was once again in the fishing grounds, and again a severe storm came up. They could see a Norwegian brig, the *O'Hansborg*, drifting, a dismasted hulk. It had collided during the night with the three-masted bark *Oscar*, which had sunk immediately. The crew was able to climb aboard the *O'Hansborg* which, thanks to its cargo of lumber, had managed to stay afloat. Again, it was Léonce and Eugène who, from their lifeboat, managed to pass a rope to the *O'Hansborg* and tow it with its seventeen men to Ostend.

"For these heroic rescues, His Majesty the King of Sweden and Norway awarded the two men the gold medal for rescue, accompanied by a letter of praise in His Majesty's own hand. For his part, His Majesty the King of the Belgians, by a decree of August 14, 1886, also bestowed on them the Civic Cross.

"Not long after this, during the course of still another fishing expedition, the *Degrave*'s coal bunker caught fire. In spite of the brothers' efforts, the fire spread and consumed the entire ship, but the men were able to get away in the lifeboat. As the ship was not insured, their loss was total.

"Their mother bought them another small sailing ship, the *Tib-Doig*, which they also used for fishing, but it, too, had a short life. A rip in the mainsail led to a wreck on the Shetland Islands in October 1887. This time, the Degraves were completely ruined. But they did not give up the sailor's life: Léonce set sail as first mate on the steamship *Shelde*, bound for the Congo (1887), and later on board the *John-Best*.

"Eugène was fortunate to get a berth as a simple sailor on the *San Andrew*, its destination Philadelphia, and Saint-Louis du Rhone on the return trip.

"Thereafter, they sailed on the *Hesperides*, the *Lord Raglan*, the *Andreta*, and the *North West*. They stopped off in San Francisco long enough to take courses at the Taylor School, which prepared those sailors with sufficient general education and practical experience for the certificate of "master of foreign trade." They apparently left San Francisco in a hurry, having come by the sloop *Minerva*—no one quite knows how—on which they arrived in Jaluit in the Marshall Islands in 1889. They sold the ship there.

"From Jaluit, they went to Japan as auxiliary sailors on the German gunboat *Wolf*, and from there to England and then Ostend, where they had a brief visit with their mother. In April 1890, they returned to London just in time for a seamen's strike. The crews would not allow foreign sailors on ships flying the British flag, so a stevedore provided them with false papers—a not uncommon practice in those days—made out to British citizens, Alexander and Joseph Rorick. Since both men spoke English like natives, the subterfuge went undetected.

"They set sail for Port Natal on the steamship *Umlazi*, and from there to Sydney on the three-masted *Raven*, but as able seamen, not as officers. It was also as sailors that they sailed on the *Vagabond* for Penrhyn, which they left for Rarotonga on the *Jessie Nicholls*."

End of saga. We are now back at the starting point. What the interrogation should have found out before the trial began had finally come to light—a true epic of the sea whose annals record few such heroic exploits.

These accounts were confirmed and amplified by different witnesses: the harbormaster at Antwerp; officers in the merchant marine who had sailed with the brothers; simple sailors and even a cook who had sailed with them on a ship around Cape Horn. They all asserted that the brothers were conscientious and devoted sailors, that no one had ever had reason to complain of their professional comportment, and that they had always been excellent companions. Even the statements in the *Vagabond*'s logbook were contested by a Liverpool sailor named George Palmer, who wrote to the British consul in Brest in a style that, while lacking polish, had the virtue of picturesque authenticity. It read:

9th of January 1894

Dear Mr. Consul

Coming home from a voyage, I have read in an English paper that two brothers called Rorick have been condemned to death for piracy.

I have known those two chaps for I was their shipmate aboard the *Vagabond* on their voyage to Penrhyn. The papers talked much about the crew having been poisoned by those two men. Now that's a lie let me tell you dear Sir. They were the nicest jolly good fellows as ever trod a ship's deck. Although we suffered much on the *Vagabond* (which was very leaky) through her bad provisions, we finished the voyage.

The two Roricks, Joe and Aleck as their name is properly written, left us in Penrhyn, but did not desert. If the master,

Mr. Robinson, reported them as deserters, it can only be because he wanted to cheat them out of their wages, and he was mean enough to do so.

As for the poisoning, all hands aft have been sick on a Sunday for having partaken of rotten preserved meat, but none of us in the forecastle have ever been ill, because we never had these provisions given to us.

You can make whatever use you like or think fit of this letter and I beg to let you know that those two old shipmates of mine were not common sailors. They were well educated, everyone could see, they were of a musical turn of mind and spoke several languages.

Every one aboard the *Vagabond* was highly pleased with them. I am awfully sorry to have lost sight of the rest of the crew who would certainly have said as I do.

I was stunned when I learned their fate as I can hardly believe that they were men to do such dirty work as killing any member of a crew either black or white.

Your most obedient servant dear Consul

George Palmer late A.B. of the *Vagabond*
Coffee Palace, Lime Street, Liverpool

It is not difficult to conjure up this old "black ball," * sitting at a table at the Coffee Palace, penning his heartfelt prose with a large clumsy hand.

Then there was the testimony of their mother, sister and brother, who naturally refused to believe in the men's guilt, and moving statements like the one addressed to Maître de Chamaillard by a friend of Eugène:

* The name given to foulmouthed and daring sailors who worked on ships belonging to an English company that had a black ball sewn in the middle of its main topsail.

Sir,

The misfortune which has befallen your client has caused me great pain. Up to now, I have refused to believe that the man accused of the *Niuroahiti*'s crime could be Eugène Degrave.

Now that the course of the trial is no longer in doubt, I feel it my duty to state that I count Eugène Degrave among my most devoted friends. I have known him for almost fifteen years and my affection for him has continued to grow, because of the very integrity and honesty of his character.

My conscience rebels at the thought that he could have committed the heinous crime of which he is accused and I suffer to see him so unhappy.

I therefore ask you, sir, to inform him of my unshakeable attachment, and I beg you to add my name to those petitioning the President of the French Republic to take my poor friend's fate under his protection.

Dr. Léon Canines,
Doctor at the Hôpital Elizabeth, Antwerp.

It would appear that everybody who had known the brothers before the tragic event not only admired them but could not imagine their ever becoming murderers. It is extraordinary that such a disparate group of people having nothing in common, no point of contact—like the sailor on the *Vagabond* and the doctor at the Hôpital Elizabeth—should in their different ways express exactly the same sentiments.

To be fair, it must be admitted that Léonce's dossier did include six charges of assault and battery, made by the Tribunal at Bruges in 1885, 1886 and 1887. This confirmed what was previously known: that "Alexander Rorique," under various circumstances, had revealed a violent nature.

The naval judiciary finally decided to summon the two men from the prison at Pontaniou and interrogate them again. They had already admitted to the name Degrave instead of Rorique, and the woman who had recognized Eugène as he was passing through Recouvrance was none other than Pauline Cloaguen, a former servant in their mother's house in Ostend.

The Tribunal wished to know why the brothers had been so stubborn about revealing their true identities. This they explained in a letter to the Port Admiral:

Sir:

When we were taken to Brest to be interrogated, it was under the name of Rorique.

When we arrived, we wanted to keep that name even though it was not our real name; we had no crime to hide, sir, but we did have an unhappy family, especially our poor mother, and we didn't want her dishonored by having her name dragged before the Tribunal.

We knew that the mystery surrounding the name Rorique would be damaging for us. On the other hand, we knew that if I, Léonce Degrave, appeared before the Naval Tribunal, my chest gleaming with the Belgian Cross, the Norwegian Gold Cross, and three other Belgian medals, all for acts of courage and devotion; that if my brother Eugène had also come before the court wearing the same cross, won at the age of nineteen, and the Norwegian Gold Cross, our judges would have placed greater faith in our account of the events; the prosecution would not have treated us like buccaneers or escaped convicts, but we would rather lose our honor and even our lives under a pseudonym than bring sorrow to our mother, whom we love.

Léonce Degrave–Eugène Degrave
Sentenced to death under the name Rorique

The two men continued to be objects of amazement and, admittedly, considerable admiration. An anonymous and awful death, accepted with classical stoicism out of love for a mother, was worthy of Plutarch's heroes. In France, the public was momentarily distracted by the bomb thrown by the anarchist Vaillant into the Chamber of the Palais Bourbon; but in Belgium, the revelation of the brothers' identities aroused intense emotion, and their conviction was taken both as an injustice and a national affront.

The press was unanimous in denouncing what it called the "irregularities" and "scandalous prejudice" of the Tribunal in Brest. After writing a passionate article in the *Chronique de Bruxelles,* one Professor Chome elected himself president of a Committee for the Defense of the Degrave Brothers, whose goal was the reversal of the sentence and liberation of the two men. Each of its seven members was carefully selected for his personality, social position, personal fortune or relatives. All were Belgian except one, Jules Texier, a lawyer recently settled in Châtellerault, who had previously practiced in Tahiti, where he was a member of the County Council. In fact, he had met the two brothers there and even had them to his house. He had been married to the sister of Léonce Brault, publisher of the *Messager de Tahiti,* and left the country when he was divorced. His acquaintance with the cast of characters and the particular quality of life in Papeete proved very useful to the committee.

Now the great question was what the naval judiciary would do next. Would it set aside the verdict of December 8 so that the accused could be tried in another jurisdiction—as would be done today? That is not the course it followed in 1894. The severity of the judges in Brest had been partly due to the fact that they were convinced that the Roriques had led checkered, crime-ridden lives, and that was the reason they had hidden their identities. But now they discovered that the brothers had a remarkable service record, studded with acts of heroism and selfless devotion.

How to reconcile such contradictory elements? How to explain the fact that after saving the lives of over thirty sailors, they could turn around and kill six others in cold blood? This would suggest that something had happened during the course of their lives which suddenly and profoundly affected their behavior. Why didn't the naval judiciary examine this facet of the crime and try to explain it?

Looking back, one can see various possibilities: In spite of the great difference in their ages—maybe even because of this difference—the brothers had always been extraordinarily close. Their affection for each other was reinforced by a common passion—their love of the sea. It is easy to imagine their happiness and pride when they were sailing their own boat in the North Sea and how deeply its loss affected them. Not only were their hopes dashed; they had lost a cherished possession. Of the two, Léonce was the more profoundly wounded. This we know from Eugène's description of the experience:

"Léonce was pale and depressed. In the light of the fire, I could see his eyes gleaming. I spoke to him. He didn't answer. He seemed not to hear. He was watching the flames creeping up, licking the tackle, devouring the ropes, making the tar sputter. I could see him moving back, step by step. He seemed to be challenging the flames as they swept down the deck under his feet. I begged him to leave the ship. He shook his head without answering. I had to leave him for a moment to berate one of our men who was about to cast off and leave without us. At that moment, I caught a terrible look on my brother's face. I read in his eyes that he wanted to throw himself into the flames headfirst and die there. I leapt at him, grabbed him around the waist and dragged him away.

"We rowed about two hundred yards and stopped there, dazed, watching the sad sight of our ship on fire.

"It was only then that I knew *how much I loved my ship!* It was one of the great tragedies of my life. I felt as if something were being torn from me. It hurt, it hurt deeply to see that inert thing consuming itself as it burned.

"We were losing everything—our fortune and our hopes. But that wasn't all. It was the *Degrave* that was disappearing, that ship I had come to love the way other men love a woman. Yes, I loved it, and it broke my heart to lose it. Poor friend! It burned to the waterline and that was the end. There were two sharp explosions: a water barrel went, and as the winch fell into the hold, it caused a strange echo in the midst of that awful noise. It was like the last farewell of our dying friend. I watched what remained of our ship disappear, then we were left in total darkness. I cried . . . One adores to suffer for what one loves."

Yet they would have had little difficulty replacing the *Degrave,* precisely because of their rescues and their indifference to financial reward. Had they been able to bring any one of the abandoned ships safely back to port, they could have claimed it as a "prize of the sea," half of whose value legally goes to its rescuers. But the *Pieter* sank virtually under their feet, and their commendable rescue of the crew did them out of their booty. As for the *O'Hansborg,* the mercantile tribunal in Antwerp decided that since its crew had remained on board, it was simply a matter involving towage on the high seas. Acknowledging their arduous efforts, the tribunal compensated the brothers to the tune of three thousand francs, specifying, however—what irony!—that the sum be shared with the entire crew, in other words, with the very men who had refused to carry a towline to the foundering ship.

In spite of all these disappointments and his family's pleas, Léonce refused to give up the sailor's life and Eugène followed him without a moment's hesitation. But from then on, they found it almost impossible to sail together. With his lieutenant's commission in the merchant marine, Léonce was able to sail aboard a steamship going to the Congo. All Eugène could get was a sailor's berth on a ship bound for Philadelphia. During this period, most Belgian ships operated under German captains who preferred having other Germans under them. Having failed to get his "master of foreign trade" certificate, Léonce had no way of getting on any of these ships. And when they took the name of Rorick and by the same token became British subjects, neither could sail except as lowly sailors.

While there was little official concern for the civilian status of ordinary sailors, officers had to establish their nationality and the validity of their commissions. And so it was as simple sailors that the brothers boarded the *Vagabond* bound for Sydney.

To be ordered about when one should be the one giving the orders must be galling. So, when a foulmouthed Australian bosun ordered Léonce to swab the deck as if he were a novice, he got a firm refusal and an unequivocal snub. In earlier days, the bosun had the power to challenge such affronts. But such were Léonce's strength and size, and the influence he and his brother exerted on the men quartered in the forecastle, that the bosun beat a retreat to the stern, causing its occupants to take fright. Many a mutiny has been known to begin in just such a way.

The brothers' possible motivation was given its most pungent interpretation by an old sea captain who had known them well in Papeete before they set sail on the doomed *Niuroahiti*. The author, René La Bruyere, met Captain Arnaud in 1923 and recorded their conversation in his book *Les Fréres Rorique*. But first, he made the following comment on the brothers' "strange mentality": "These are figures out of the Old Testament. They carried inside them the seeds of good and evil. Because they had deprived the ocean of thirty-seven lives, they believed they were empowered to give it back seven dead. They were larger than life even in their crimes."

Then La Bruyère quotes Arnaud: "With strapping men

like these, you have to remember that the poor human race is a paradoxical mixture of virtues and vices. There is nothing more like a hero than a pirate of the Roriques' stamp. Had it been up to me, I would have granted them mitigating circumstances."

La Bruyère was dumbfounded. "For this monstrous act of piracy!"

"Yes, because it was a crime of passion." La Bruyère was too stunned to reply; Arnaud continued: "Have you considered the Roriques' motives? You think they killed seven people to get their hands on a few thousand piasters? Obviously not." La Bruyère looked doubtful; Arnaud went on: "You make allowances for a man who has committed murder out of love for a woman. Well, the Roriques committed murder out of love for the sea. The sea is every bit as worthy as a woman!

"To understand a pirate's soul you have to have commanded a schooner as I did, and known the joy of feeling yourself the master—second only to God—of a pretty little cockleshell giving herself to the trade winds like a mistress. You have to have penetrated into the lagoons under the dazzling tropical sun, and come about within feet of the edge of a coral reef or risk being smashed up and killed. And finally, you have to have plucked a *vahine* of the archipelagos like a flower. These sensations can explain a murder even if they don't justify it."

Arnaud stopped and picked an oyster shell from his collection which still cradled a perfect pearl. With a flick of the finger, he freed the pearl and threw the empty shell into the bushes. "This is the heart of our adventurers. It took one simple shock to loosen the pearl. All that remained was the ravished jewel box."

Maupin was not interested in the brothers' psychological condition, and besides, he was far too preoccupied with other matters: How was the naval judiciary going to come out of the affair with its honor intact? Inevitably, a second trial would bring a new horde of journalists to Brest, not only from France, but from Belgium and probably England and Germany as well. Moreover, one of the members of the Committee for the Defense of the Degrave Brothers was a Van den Cruyssen, whose family had an enormous fortune. The committee was sure to retain the services of one of the best lawyers in Paris before whom a Compristo or a Maupin would carry little weight. The navy ran the risk of inviting abuse and even ridicule.

Maupin conveyed his anxiety to the Port Admiral, adding that, if necessary, he was willing—as Crespin had been— to claim his rights to retirement. Certainly not! He must stay at his post; it was an order. Never mind the fact that it was his careless performance that had prevented the brothers' identity from being discovered before the trial. Meanwhile, further instructions were sought from the Minister of the Navy, Félix Faure.

On March 3, 1894, the First Naval Tribunal convened once again and summoned the brothers to appear before it. It was a short session for, when all was said and done, all it had to deal with was the matter of their identities.

Just two questions were asked: "Was there a connection between the so-called Joseph Rorique and Eugène Degrave?" and: "Was there a connection between the so-called Alexander Rorique and Léonce Degrave?"

The Tribunal's answers were affirmative. The President then read the decision: "The government prosecutor requests that if it please the permanent First Naval Tribunal of the port of Brest, it rectify the verdict of December 8, 1893, and state that it applies equally to Messrs. Eugène Degrave and Léonce Degrave. And it furthermore orders that, apart from the above verdict, this rectification be made wherever else it may be necessary."

That was all.

France was stupefied; Belgium was indignant.

Séverine, the well-known woman activist, immediately took up the Degraves' cause—although she persisted in calling them Rorique—and wrote a letter of protest to Waldeck Rousseau, the President du Conseil (the upper house of the French Parliament). In the press, she fulminated against "the misdeeds of a special court in the hands of a military clique."

In his newspaper *La Justice*, Georges Clemenceau printed an even more vitriolic article under the title: "An Error of Justice." He, too, attacked "that disguised court-martial which, in defiance of all laws, smothered the defense and committed a series of irregularities."

A few months later, in December 1894, a court-martial charged a certain Captain Dreyfus with treason, which unleased an unprecedented flood of passions throughout France. The verdict of the Tribunal in Brest was in a sense a prelude to the more celebrated "Dreyfus Affair."

Meanwhile, the *Chronique de Bruxelles* raised the question to a national level when it disclosed that during the session on March 3, the Naval Tribunal had refused to make public a letter written by Baron Bayen, the Belgian

Ambassador in Paris and dean of the diplomatic corps. The *Chronique* called on the Belgian government to seek amends to the affront. As tempers flared in Brussels, Baron Bayen was permitted an audience with Sadi Carnot. The Foreign Office, alarmed by the reports of Belgian hostility toward France, gently reminded the Elysée that since it was the policy of the French government, as it was Britain's, to recognize and guarantee Belgium's neutrality, it must *at all costs* maintain and preserve the best relations possible with that country.

Only the Head of State, with his right to grant pardons, was in a position to calm the people's passions. Taking its cue from Maupin's report, the committee on pardons gave an unfavorable verdict and the President of the Republic was supposed never to go against the verdicts of this committee. Nevertheless, throwing tradition to the winds, Sadi Carnot signed the Degraves' pardon on March 13, 1894.

Reasons of state always take precedence over justice . . .

IX

ON MARCH 18, after a hundred days of anguished waiting, the Degrave brothers were informed by Maupin that their sentences had been commuted. For him, as for the First Naval Tribunal, the presidential pardon granted in the face of their unfavorable ruling was the equivalent of an insult.

In the dossier of "L'Affaire Rorique," filed away in the historical archives of the navy, there is a letter from Gabriel Hanotaux, the then Minister of Foreign Affairs, to Félix Faure, Minister of the Navy. It is a significant letter, obviously written by Hanotaux himself, and for all its flourishes and carefully honed diplomatic jargon, the minister could not quite conceal his irritation. Hanotaux wished to remind his colleague that, in pursuit of France's well-known policy, he had succeeded in detaching Italy from the Triple Alliance, and he solemnly proclaimed once again France's and Britain's guarantee of Belgium's neutrality. How then, in view of these conditions, had the Minister of the Navy failed to understand that he must intervene in the "stupid" trial in Brest because it was threatening Franco-Belgian relations at the precise moment when they were most necessary?

Had the case been brought before a British court, the lack of clear and evident proof would have brought a verdict of hard labor for life rather than the death penalty. President Carnot's decision was certainly influenced as much by diplomatic imperatives as by personal conviction. The Brest Tribunal's obstinate refusal to admit its blunders, not to say errors, aroused a considerable body of public opinion.

The two convicts, now transferred to a civil jurisdiction, were taken to the fort at Bouguen. As a first indication of their fall from grace, their hair, beards and mustaches were shaved off. After a few days, they were moved to the depot at the Ile de Ré, where convoys of convicts destined for Guiana and New Caledonia were assembled.

Léonce and Eugène were about to make their first acquaintance with a civilian jail, with its filth, pettiness, Corsican guards, informers, and systematic degradation. By comparison, the prison at Pontaniou seemed like an Eden they had failed to appreciate. Yet even there, they almost victimized the warden, "the excellent Compredon," as Eugène himself called him. This fact came recently to light in a letter written by Léonce three days after the verdict, to a certain M. de la Ménardière, a shipchandler and outfitter in Brest who, convinced of their innocence like so many others, had expressed his sympathy during the trial. By a curious coincidence, this letter turned up in a dictionary belonging to la Ménardière's son eighty years after it was written. During the course of the long letter, Léonce wrote:

"Do I dare tell you . . . we have thought up a plan of escape. Yes, there are ways we can get outside the Pontaniou walls on a given evening, *without having to use violence*. But once there, what should we do, where can we go? The population knows us, we have no friends, no one to help us, and the only clothes we have are those we wore in the courtroom or our prison uniforms. We must be able to go immediately to a place where a friend can hide us for a day or two, but alas, we have no friends. It is true that the people are sympathetic, but not to the point of giving us protection.

"That is why, sir, when we saw from your excellent letter how well disposed you were toward us, that we thought of you. You have steamboats going to England. One word from you to the captain would be enough to save us.

"Could you be so hard-hearted as to refuse us asylum if we turned up at your door one night and placed our lives in your hands? Any kind of shelter, a piece of bread, a drink of water would do while we waited until we could hide on board one of your ships."

There is no record of M. de la Ménardière's reply to this strange proposal, doomed to certain failure. Later, Eugène stated that under no conditions would he have allowed himself to die ignominiously under the guillotine's knife; the executioner and his aides would have found only corpses in their cells. Actually, both men carried enough cyanide of potassium—carefully camouflaged and hermetically sealed in tinfoil—to kill ten men. How had they come by this poison? Perhaps the explanation lies in their proximity to the port's ironworks and foundries, where the product was used to case-harden steel.

At the depot on the Ile de Ré, a guard offered Eugène the job of foreman overseeing the teams of convicts working in a shop belonging to a private operator. Eugène refused him contemptuously, saying he was no stool pigeon. A heated exchange followed, during which the guard decided he had been insulted and possibly threatened. This earned Eugène a spell in solitary confinement, but Léonce was allowed to be in the same cell, which helped mitigate the punishment. At night, each man had one foot chained to a bar attached to their cots.

Meanwhile, the Committee for the Defense was far from inactive. It was able to obtain an audience with President Carnot for the Degraves' mother and sister. The poor mother flung herself at the President's knees and he promised he would use the occasion of the French national holiday on July 14th to announce another act of clemency.

The Committee also obtained permission to visit the brothers on the Ile de Ré. The men were let out of their cells and the guards were suddenly overflowing with good will. True, the Committee had distributed a quantity of cigars to the guards and ordered them an excellent meal at the island's only hotel.

As another result of the presidential interview, Léonce and Eugène were posted to the office for new arrivals, a real "cushy job," in the convicts' view. That is how it came about that, working to assemble a convoy due to leave the island on July 13, they often crossed paths with ex-Captain Dreyfus, who was likewise on his way to l'Ile du Diable. The brothers were to be in the same convoy, but thanks to its influence in high places, the Committee was able to defer their departure until after the President's announcement.

The Committee was resolutely optimistic when the news came that President Carnot had been assassinated on June 24—again an anarchist's victim. For the Degraves, it was a mortal blow.

The Committee was forced to begin all over again with the new President, Casimir Périer, but he abruptly resigned after only a few months in office, and Félix Faure, of all people, was elected President on January 19, 1895. This time, all hope was abandoned. It was Félix Faure who, as Minister of the Navy, had given special instructions that the brothers not be retried, and that the verdict against the Roriques be applied to the Degraves.

The Committee was even fearful that the naval judiciary would make the brothers pay for its humiliation during Carnot's presidency. The brothers' request for a transfer to New Caledonia, heretofore viewed with favor, was turned down with the notation: "Under no circumstances will they be sent to the Pacific, scene of their criminal exploits." And "since they loved the sea so much," they would be deported to Guiana—the Iles du Salut—where escape was all but impossible.

There was nothing left for the brothers but to swallow their disappointment and resentment. Eugène especially had it in for everybody: Mirey, naval justice, the guards, even the Belgian government which had done everything in its power to save them from the guillotine. Gratitude was not his strong point. In an angry letter to his brother Auguste, written from Saint Martin-de-Ré on July 17, 1895, he said:

My dear Auguste,

A few moments after mailing you the letter I wrote on July 14th, I was told that I'd been chosen to leave for Guiana. The departure is scheduled for the 25th of this month. I was overjoyed. I was very excited to be leaving this terrible place where I've suffered so much for a full year and four months. Then came your letter of the 13th, plunging me into a long and cruel wait. Why should I be kept here for more months on end? It's enough to drive a man mad, but then I don't know why I haven't gone mad long before this! If the Belgian government had really asked that we be sent to New Caledonia, we would gladly have gone, for they grant this favor to the worst murderers, let alone ordinary people like us. Even more reason to grant it to a government, but there's no ship leaving for New Caledonia for six or seven months! That means spending another winter here! Can you imagine the horror of our position! Just thinking about it makes me tremble. What business is it of the Belgian government? What right have they to ask that we get better treatment in Cayenne? Have we complained about the treatment in Cayenne? If the Belgian government is suddenly taking such interest in two men it shamefully repudiated, not to say betrayed, why didn't it try to find out how we were being treated here!

Before it beholds the mote in the French government's eye, let the Belgian government consider the beam in its own! If we'd been accorded what we deserved for the rescue of the *Van Iseghen,* and if during August of last year, the Belgian government had had the courage of its convictions, we would certainly not be here now. It had the opportunity then to make a public protest on our behalf, if only in the line of duty! August is coming again soon. Do you believe the Belgian government is going to make amends? No. So why is it sticking its nose into this affair? Let them busy themselves about

[170]

Belgianizing the negroes in the Congo and leave us in peace. What right have they to prolong our agony for another six or seven months? It's clear we need an honest enemy more than a stupid friend. As for getting us a pardon, I beg you, dear Auguste, don't fall into that trap. Haven't you proof enough already that we'll never have an hour's pardon?

On July 26, 1895, Eugène's sad dreams were realized: the brothers were assigned to the convict ship *Ville de Saint-Nazaire*. As they had been labeled "especially dangerous individuals by reason of their intelligence and physical strength," they were the last on board and were flanked by eight guards whom Eugène later described as "a royal escort."

The *Ville de Saint-Nazaire*, a 1500-ton steamboat belonging to the Nantes Navigation Company, was periodically requisitioned by the State for the transportation of convicts to Guiana. The convicts were divided up into different compartments in steerage called *bagnes* (as were the penitentiaries themselves), which were partitioned off by grills of thick iron bars. They looked like animal cages in the circus, and smelled like them too, especially when bad weather forced the closing of the main hatchway.

The only furniture consisted of simple wooden benches attached to the bulkheads three feet above the floor. At night, the occupants slept in hammocks hooked to the deck beams which were stuffed into sacks during the day. Their food was basically the same as the sailors'.

As they came aboard, Eugène and Léonce suddenly had a feeling of well-being, almost of peace: they were back on the deck of a ship! But they were soon separated,

Eugène in a *bagne* in the bow, Léonce in the stern. They were viewed with particular suspicion at sea. But at the same time, their reputation as pirates gave them special prestige and authority among convicts whose experience of the sea was limited.

It was the brothers who saw to the maintenance of order and cleanliness, and as a result, their respective *bagnes* looked more like well-kept sailors' quarters than a prison ship. They showed the men how to hang their hammocks so that they would sleep more comfortably, gave advice here, a reprimand there. The guards were dumbfounded.

The *Saint-Nazaire*'s crew was equally impressed by the tidiness of their cages, for usually, when the weather was bad, the men became seasick and lay on the tweendeck in the midst of indescribable filth and squalor.

When the ship entered the tropics, life in the *bagne* became particularly difficult. The sun beat down on the hull's metal plate and with the wind blowing steadily from the stern, the temperature in the cages often reached 120 degrees, making sleep almost impossible. A one hour's recess on deck and a watering down with sea water from a firehose were the only pleasant moments of the day.

After fourteen days at sea, the *Ville de Saint-Nazaire* dropped anchor off the Isles du Salut, eight miles from the coast and fifteen miles from Cayenne. The three rocky islands formed a cloverleaf: l'Ile Royale where most of the convicts lived; l'Ile Saint-Joseph, also called l'Ile du Silence, where the convicts condemned to the horror of solitary confinement were confined; and finally, l'Ile du Diable, the political prisoners' camp. Ex-Captain Dreyfus was already there, watched over day and night by shifts of four guards to whom he never addressed a word.

The Iles du Salut were used only for those convicts assumed to be dangerous or suspected of intentions to escape. These also included men who had incurred punishment in the camp at Saint-Laurent du Maroni, headquarters of the penitential administration. In a manner of speaking, the Iles du Salut were reserved for the "upper crust" among the convicts.

As soon as the *Ville de Saint-Nazaire* arrived, Boucher, the islands' chief warden, went aboard to review his new contingent. Eugène's size and general appearance made him stand out over the rest of his companions, many of whom bore the unmistakable stamp of criminals.

"That man makes a good impression," Boucher said to Le Goff, the guard standing by him—a former sailor and a decent man when he wasn't drunk.

"His number is 27,029, and I can tell you he made the trip a lot easier for me. You should have seen how well his quarters were kept. He was the boss down there; he gave orders and everybody obeyed."

"What's his name?"

"Eugène Degrave."

The warden was startled. "What did you say? Isn't that one of the 'brothers'?"

He glanced at Eugène again, this time with less enthusiasm. "I don't like convicts who exercise authority over others. I break the 'big-shots'," he said, clamping his cap down over his eyes, and concluded the inspection then and there.

A few minutes later, Eugène and Léonce were taken

off the boat. Eugène was dismayed when he saw that Léonce was being taken to Saint-Joseph while he was going to Royale. Once there, he was locked up in solitary confinement and chained at night. His cell was tiny, dark, filthy and stiflingly hot. Centipedes, scorpions and poisonous spiders scuttled about everywhere; because of the islands' proximity to land, they had inherited all of Guiana's vermin, including its snakes.

After a certain number of days had passed, Eugène began to wonder if Boucher intended to forget him. If that were the case, he preferred to die. Then, one morning, the cell door was suddenly thrown open.

"Eh, you in there! You think you're going to spend your days doing nothing?" The guard threw him an old straw hat and ordered him to join a work gang. Eugène was relieved to be out of his stinking hole, even though he was back in chains every night.

At that time, a jetty was being built on l'Ile Royale with rocks quarried on the island. The methods used were unbelievably primitive: a simple wooden lever made of hardwood with a steel head served to split the rock and move it about. The convicts called it "the pencil." No explosives were used, for the convicts might smuggle them out and use them for making escapes. The blocks were transported on a cart pulled by thirty men in breast harnesses. The results were ludicrously slim, but what did it matter? The main object was "make-work," and Eugène had the impression he was Sisyphus.

When, in 1852, the *bagnes* in Brest and Toulon were closed down, the authorities decided to send all convicts to Guiana. They had high hopes that penal labor would help develop a virtually unknown country, much of which was covered with virgin forests. To achieve this end, a law passed in May 1854 gave various urban and rural concessions to those convicts who had fulfilled certain conditions. The convicts lived in partial freedom, received a small salary for the fruits of their labors, and despite the shocking death rate, their production continued to grow and prosper. It also contributed to the *bagne*'s food supply in the form of tapioca, rice, sweet potatoes and even meat.

This lasted until 1891, when a new decree undid the good work of forty years, depriving the convicts of the right to receive compensation for their work. The official charged with explaining the reasons for the law clearly knew nothing about the *bagne* or working conditions there. In his words, "How can society pay a convict for work that constitutes his punishment?" This of course was pure theory. In practice, the application of the decree brought an immediate drop in production. After a few years, the penitential establishment could no longer depend on local produce and was forced increasingly to rely on imports. As a result, the cost of feeding the convicts grew rapidly, the amount of food was cut down, and on the Iles du Salut it became shockingly insufficient. The men were expected to do heavy work on reduced rations whose quality and quantity were a disgrace.

Eugène and his work gang were building a small fort on l'Ile du Diable to guard Dreyfus. To their delight, they discovered on arriving each morning that the ex-captain had left them some bread on a low wall. (Dreyfus was in fact receiving food from his family through a shopkeeper in Cayenne.) Then, one day, a guard happened upon the collusion, seized the bread and fed it to the chickens. From that moment on, the *bagne* was bent on revenge.

After two months at hard labor, Eugène—to his astonishment—was transferred to the kitchens. It was the easiest of all the jobs available and he couldn't at first understand the reason for his good fortune. He learned soon enough that one of the cooks was an official informer. Everything Eugène said, and probably much that he hadn't said, was reported to the guards, squealing being the fountainhead of the penitentiary system.

Knowing of the affection between the two brothers, the authorities gave strict orders that they be kept separated. They assumed that, no matter what the circumstances, neither would try to escape without the other.

Ten months after their arrival, Eugène and Léonce happened to run into each other as one gang was relieving another. They fell into each other's arms, but the guard watching the scene forbade them to speak any language but French. Eugène was shocked by his brother's appearance and at how thin and old he'd grown. He was careful not to make any comment, but Léonce's condition distressed him greatly.

Eugène was not considering escape at the time, but he was made party to all the plans under discussion—some of them of course pure folly—and being a sailor, his advice was much sought after. He gave it freely, improved or corrected poorly conceived plans, and plotted with such ardor that people thought he must be planning his own escape.

The head warden on the Iles du Salut had a sturdy clinker-built yawl manned by six convicts. Confiding in

Eugène, the rowers outlined a plan of escape: they would wait for the moment the guard's attention was diverted by his disembarking, then row with all their might out to sea. Eugène pointed out that the island's steam launch could easily overtake them, but as it was periodically beached when the hull needed scraping, that would be the moment to execute their plan.

The occasion presented itself one day when the guard using the yawl wished to visit the warden, and ordered the men to wait for him alongside the wharf. The boat moved gently away, then rowing in synchronized rhythm, the men steered her toward the channel separating Royale from Saint Joseph. Going west was out of the question, for they would have to pass close to a schooner unloading merchandise that was being watched by three armed guards.

As soon as the alarm sounded, guards came running from all directions and started shooting at the fugitives. Word of the escape made the rounds of the camp like brush fire. It was noon, and the convicts were eating lunch in a hangar with barred windows. A cluster of men gathered at each window, egging the rowers on in their fantastic race as the rifle shots rang out. Eugène, transported with excitement, was yelling: "Not so fast! Not so fast! Don't break your rhythm!" as if the men could hear him. Bullets were raining down around the yawl, sending up little white geysers of water. A piece of the gunwale broke off and exploded into a thousand pieces, but none of the men seemed to have been hit. It was an exciting spectacle to see them rowing as if they were in a regatta. A Sister of Saint-Vincent de Paul who worked at the hospital, happened to pass by at that moment. Turning pale, she murmured: "Oh, my God! Oh, my God!" Then, suddenly, a great roar went up from all the barracks: "They've made it! Hurray! They've gotten through!" The boat had reached the channel and was heading for the open sea. The head warden requisitioned the schooner moored in the port, and took a dozen soldiers armed with Lebel rifles that had a much longer range than the guards' Gras. The anchor was quickly weighed, the sails hoisted and the schooner set off in a northeasterly breeze.

"If they keep going straight into the wind," Eugène said to his companions, "the schooner, which has to keep tacking, will never catch up with them or even get near them before nightfall."

The fugitives' boat could still be clearly seen, heading for the open sea. Suddenly, Eugène let out a cry: "What are they doing? They can't be . . . They're mad! They're heading toward land!"

Eugène wrung his hands in anger and despair. "That finishes it," he said sadly. "They're good rowers but they're not sailors. They shouldn't have been afraid of a heavy tub that can't tack properly. They should have kept on going at all costs. Now they're done for."

The yawl was heading for Kourou, the schooner reached into a strong following wind and arrived near shore at almost the same moment as the fugitives. All the men were caught and brought back to the islands the next morning, tied together like sausages, including two wounded. Their punishment: a year in solitary in "special quarters."

Eugène's remarks were reported to the authorities and it convinced them that he had been their advisor, perhaps even the instigator of the escape. As a result, he got a month in a cell on Saint-Joseph with a chain a yard long with a ball weighing seven pounds attached to his left foot. He spent a year with that chain.

The "special quarters," an administrative euphemism for the group of cells used for solitary confinement on Saint-Joseph, were particularly dreaded by the convicts. To them, they were the antechamber of death.

The convict had to endure absolute silence in a loathsome cell without air or light. He lay on asphalt, and in order to breathe during the heat of the day, he had to press his mouth against a piece of tin punctured with holes nailed to the bottom of the cell door. His nourishment was below subsistence level, and it didn't take him long to turn into the dregs of humanity, morally as well as physically. Yet such are the incredible powers of human endurance that certain men were able to survive months and even years.

During his time in solitary Eugène had ample time to consider the convicts' situation. When a self-righteous society has rid itself of these men, it has little desire to see them return at the end of their sentences. For that reason, it decreed that all sentences to hard labor be matched with residence in Guiana, five years at hard labor being the equivalent of ten years in Guiana. After seven years, the convict was compelled to stay on for life in a place where there was little hope of making a living. And were he to commit a simple offense, he would be sent back to the *bagne* for an unlimited duration. The term "dry guillotine," in use since the days of the Directoire, was the perfect expression for a method of elimination without bloodshed, although this did not prevent the real thing from being used regularly—as many as five times in one month. The convicts were made to watch every execution on their knees, but the repeated sight of the spectacle did little to mend their ways, let alone impress them.

In this hell, where informing was a way of life, and wretched Arab convicts were promoted to overseers and turnkeys, beating their charges with truncheons as they shouted "Ro Roumi!" (March, Christian!), it is little wonder that terrible acts of revenge were customary. A permanent tribunal meted out the death sentence in the space of a few hours, with no appeal, even as the sinister machine was being raised in the main courtyard. One chief warden even suggested that the machine be kept in constant readiness as a deterrent.

It is interesting to note that during this same period, a play called *De Gebroeders Degrave* ran successfully in Brussels for two years. In it, the brothers died at the hands of the guards, which brought copious tears to the eyes of a large public.

The Committee for the Defense of the Degrave Brothers was not discouraged, despite President Félix Faure's refusal to see them. At the height of the agitation over the Dreyfus case, such eminent men as Georges Clemenceau and Emile Zola recommended that the Committee merge the two cases and thereby permit a powerful attack on the tribunals and military justice in general. At first blush, the Committee was taken with the proposition, but it later declined to go ahead. Auguste, writing to Eugène and Léonce, in January 1897, said: "I refused to permit it," but gave no reason. What had happened?

It is possible that the French government, not eager to

see an already perilous situation get out of hand, made certain promises to the Committee. On June 28, 1897, the President of the Republic signed a decree commuting the brothers' life sentence to twenty years at hard labor. This was the very same man who had ensured the sentence of capital punishment made by the Naval Tribunal in Brest.

Eugène and Léonce did not fully appreciate this act of clemency. On the contrary, Eugène saw it as a cruel trick because their new sentence went into effect only from that day on; the four years already served counted for nothing.

At about the same time, the *Cymbelline*, a schooner from Cayenne, unloaded a cargo of sand on l'Ile Saint-Joseph. Although Eugène was classed among the "incorrigibles," he was put in charge of the unloading because of his experience. Ristori, the guard on duty, ordered seventeen men into the *Cymbelline*'s longboat, a boat with a normal capacity of eight. Eugène commented on the fact, but the guard turned a deaf ear and shoved the boat off. It hadn't gone thirty yards when water began to flow over the gunwales, the boat began filling, and capsized. The men floundered in the water while Eugène reached the wharf in a few strokes. But when he looked back, he saw that some of the men couldn't swim and were about to drown.

As he ripped off his clothes and dove into the water, a cry went up: "A shark!" Sure enough, a triangular fin could be seen circling the boat. Since available land was very scarce on the Iles du Salut, when convicts died, they were thrown into the sea. And although sharks preferred other fish, they had ended up taking a liking to human flesh.

One man, in a fit of panic, seized Eugène by the neck when he tried to help him. He finally freed himself, hauled the man into the capsized boat and towed it to shore, the chain stopper clamped between his teeth. When he reached the wharf, Ristori was moved to say: "That was a very good thing you did."

The guard had already committed the serious error of letting a boatload of convicts row off without being in the boat himself. With the help of the other men, a sailor like Eugène could easily have boarded the schooner, thrown the two black sailors overboard, weighed anchor and set off. Besides, Ristori had refused to take Eugène's advice on the way to conduct the operation.

When the head guard, an Alsatian named Pfaender, arrived on the scene, he asked Eugène to bring up the picks and shovels that had gone to the bottom when the boat capsized. Eugène replied: "I don't mind risking my life to save men, but if it's for equipment belonging to the *bagne*, go get it yourself." So, for all his courage, Eugène spent that night in solitary. Actually, if Eugène had been congratulated for his bravery, Ristori in turn would have had to be blamed for his lack of responsibility.

Not long after, the brothers received the sad news of their mother's death. And then, as if the poor family hadn't suffered enough, an anonymous letter arrived, addressed to the King's counsel in Antwerp, stating that she had been poisoned by their brother Auguste. An investigation was undertaken, with an examination, exhumation of the body, the reports of experts, but none of its efforts were conclusive. The scandal, however, had a disastrous effect on Auguste and his career as a stockbroker.

Léonce's health had been deteriorating for some time; he was now hospitalized with a serious case of dysentery. When he grew steadily worse, Eugène obtained permission to visit him. "As soon as I looked at him," he wrote later, "I saw the mask of death on his face."

Léonce had no illusions about the state of his health, but he tried to act relaxed and cheerful with his brother. Three days later, Eugène was allowed back at the hospital. Léonce was in critical condition, an intestinal hemorrhage having drained him of blood. His eyes were glazed, his mind wandered, he called for his mother, and appeared not to recognize his brother. Eugène was allowed to stay by his bedside the entire day. Léonce died that evening.

Eugène broke into sobs and threw himself on his brother's emaciated body. In this place where all pity was considered outlawed, several convicts tried to comfort him and held him back when he tried to dash his head against the wall. One last painful operation still remained. At five in the morning, as the chapel bell tolled, the last rites were to be performed: Léonce's body would be thrown to the sharks. Then, a very unusual thing took place: Deniel, the chief warden on the islands, took Eugène aside and talked to him for a long time. Perhaps this otherwise inflexible and insensitive man found the right words, for Eugène suddenly sat down and cried his heart out. When he had finally calmed down, he let himself be taken to the other end of the island while his brother's body was thrown into the sea.

It may have been as consolation that Eugène was named

assistant to Argis, the bookkeeper for the colonial administration and manager of the island's general store. It was
an enviable job, but to Eugène, it was only another sign
of Deniel's Machiavellian ways. The position allowed for
leisure time and even some possibilities for escape, but by
the same token, it was hazardous employment. Since the
assistant bookkeeper was in charge of the canteen and it
was his job to distribute wine to the troops and guards, it
often happened that the dispenser of the wine drank a
bit too much himself and committed some grievous
blunder. This is precisely what had happened to Eugène's
predecessor. But in this area, Eugène thought himself safe:
"I could run a canteen for twenty years and not drink a
drop of wine." On the other hand, his desire to escape
developed into an obsession. He could think of nothing
else. With the means at his disposal, he managed to con-
struct and hide a raft in the general storeroom.

As he waited for the right moment to launch his operation—a question of coordinating both surveillance and
meteorology—news arrived of the sudden death of President Félix Faure.

The news filled Eugène with satisfaction and hope.
Auguste's letters indicated that the new President, Emile
Loubet, might consider an offer of clemency on July 14th.
But his letters also expressed concern over the vehemence
of Eugène's many resentments. Was he, at the very moment hope was rekindled, going to commit some irrepar-
able folly?

July passed, and by mid-August there was still no news
of a possible clemency. Eugène made up his mind: he
would make his escape on August 23, the night of the

new moon—for he needed a dark night if his scheme was to work. But he noticed, a few nights before the date, that the guards' nightly rounds had been speeded up. He would be a fool to try anything under these conditions. The guards were sure to shoot on sight. So he decided to postpone his attempt until September 20. On that day, he would either be free—or dead.

On September 3, he was summoned before the chief warden and handed a telegram. By a Presidential decree dated August 24, he was pardoned, a full pardon without even the obligation to do time in Guiana. Three days later, he was on the quay at Cayenne, ready to sail on the *Lafayette* bound for Saint-Nazaire.

X

THE REASONS for the Presidential pardon will always remain a mystery. At the time, it caused the widest speculation, and no version was too unlikely or irrational to merit credence.

One theory had it that the two brothers were of illustrious birth: Eugène was singled out as nothing less than the son of King Leopold II of Belgium. True, this amiable and lighthearted sovereign was known to appreciate pretty women. That was all that was needed, bearing out the saying "Those who have, get."

When he arrived in Saint-Nazaire on October 24, 1899, Eugène was greeted by Fritz Lutens, a journalist from the *Messager de Bruxelles*, who accompanied him to Paris. At Mons, on the border, he was welcomed by his brother Auguste, his two sisters, Marie and Léonie, and his brother-in-law Davin. A goodly number greeted him on the platform at Mons; in Brussels, there was a crowd, and the former convict received an ovation. The Committee for the Defense treated him like a national hero to the point where Eugène was embarrassed. For a week, he was the object of the most intense curiosity. Séverine, the French writer, made the trip to Belgium to meet him, and gave him the idea of writing his memoirs of the *bagne*. When he hesitated, she suggested she help him write it.

He set to work right away, recording every incident while it was still fresh in his memory. It was then corrected, organized into chapters and published as a three-hundred-page volume by Stock in Paris in 1901. Entitled *Le Bagne,* the book was the first to be written about the Iles du Salut, antedating the articles by the evangelical missionary Paul Richard in the *Journal du Siècle,* as well as the accounts by Albert Londres and Francis Carco. These were to create a sensation, being the first revelations of the guards' inhuman treatment of the convicts. Such was the pressure of public opinion that six decrees were passed on September 18, 1925, tempering the punishment of the condemned and controlling—up to a point—the behavior of the guards.

Although Eugène protested that he didn't know how to write, his style is clear, precise, occasionally lively, although the tone is generally polemical. He had a grudge against everybody: the Spaniards in Ponape, the officers on the *Shamrock,* the judges in Brest, and even Tahiti and its people. But his most vicious attacks were reserved for the guards at the *bagne;* oddly enough, only the police escaped his venom. The book was dedicated to Séverine, who admittedly deserved it. In his dedication, he wrote: "You will not find very literary things in my memoirs, Madame. I write the truth, such as it is, crudely. It was done as an act of justice. I've never written anything before and I've never asked for anyone's help. I know how to handle a boat better than a pen, but like a good sailor, I have feelings, I know what I admire.

"I admire you, Madame, not only for what you did for me, but for what you have done, what you are still doing for other unfortunate people."

Probably the public was not as receptive or as sensitive to the fate of convicts as we are today, and a commercial success like Charrière's *Papillon* would have been inconceivable in those days. There was only one edition of *Le Bagne*, which explains its rarity today.

Much later, when René La Bruyère had written the first story of the Rorique brothers for the weekly periodical *Gringoire*, subsequently published in book form as *Les Frères Rorique*, he received the following letter from Eugène's brother-in-law:

"I knew the survivor of that terrible tragedy in the Pacific quite well, and I have serious doubts about the veracity of that shifty Mirey who, in my view—and I have traveled to the four corners of the earth—is nothing but a negro, a liar and a thief. I have friends who lived in Papeete for twenty-five years and knew him well. They didn't have a good word to say for him; they thought he was a poor thing indeed.

"Regardless of what took place and his presumed crimes, my brother-in-law Eugène was received, I should even say fêted, in many a drawing room, both French and foreign. Also, he served the Prince of Monaco, was named chief of the harbor police in Trinidad (where I saw him in 1907), acted as head of the Costa Rican consulate in New Orleans, etc., etc. Séverine, Jacques Dhur, Loïe Fuller and her mother, the son of Casimir Périer, Mme. Heriot, and thousands of other well-known people treated him like an ill-starred child, often in my presence. This leads me to have serious doubts about the guilt of these two brave boys, as you yourself have described them. And besides, why would they have been granted full liberty if they were thought to be so dangerous?"

One witness, meeting Eugène at this time, described him as "a burly fellow with a pleasant face that contrasts oddly with his Herculean build. He has a fresh, well-shaven complexion, a mustache that turns up at the ends, his long hair is worn parted and .he dresses with care. He gives the impression of arrogance, but he has a serious and open face."

Eugène never sailed on a ship again, except as a passenger, for the obvious reason that despite the enthusiasm shown him by the Belgians at the time of his liberation, shipowners, who also read the newspapers, were not eager to take on such a notorious person.

For Eugène to have to renounce the seafarer's life must have been a bitter blow. "We were all sailors," he proudly stated in his book. "We came from a long line of sailors." To bear him out, it was discovered that a certain Captain Peter Degrave from Antwerp had been in Tasmania in 1822 and was well known in Australian waters as a big-talker and something of a fourflusher, for he had been locked up in the Hobart jail for nonpayment of debts. Could this Captain Degrave have been a great-uncle? All that is known is that he was freed on condition that he pick up a contingent of Wesleyan emigrants in England on his three-masted schooner, the *Hope*.

According to contemporary accounts, the *Hope* was

little more than a heavy "wagon" that moved slowly and constantly drifted off course. But he managed to take on the emigrants in Downs in November 1824, but because of bad weather, he had to return to his anchorage in Downs two weeks later. His crew was in a state of exhaustion, his ship leaked, and his rigging was badly damaged.

For two months, the unfortunate Wesleyans lived on the ship in the bitter cold of winter, on an open roadstead exposed to the winds, and close to starvation. They sent a delegation to see the authorities, who decided immediately that the emigrants should be taken off the ship. Captain Degrave was delighted to exchange his bigoted, nondrinking and complaining Wesleyans for a complete though dismantled brewery destined for Sydney, a much more lucrative freight than a band of missionaries.

The *Hope* continued to sail between Hobart and Sydney until it went aground on a sand bank in the Bay of Storms, thereafter known as Hope Beach.

When the crew abandoned ship, nothing was lost except a heavy oak chest bound with metal strips containing a large amount of gold coin destined for the Colonial Treasury. Two soldiers had been sent along to guard it, but it disappeared even though the ship was intact. The hull had been staved in in several places, and perhaps the precious chest had slipped out onto the sand. But the many searches conducted subsequently and even up to the present time have turned up nothing.

Eugène, meanwhile, had to earn a living, and some friends found him a job as a salesman for Malines lace—a strange fate for a dangerous pirate to end his career selling frills and furbelows.

In the course of his travels, he went often to France, where he eventually married a girl of excellent family whose brother, a ship's captain, worked in the offices of the Port of Le Havre. Soon after, a daughter was born.

But it's unthinkable that Eugène should finish his eventful life as a smug bourgeois. In 1907, he turned up in Trinidad as the port's chief of police—again, an odd post for a man who had suffered so much at their hands.

A few years later, he surfaced in the United States, in New Orleans.

XI

~~~~~~

ONE NOVEMBER MORNING in 1917—a mild day with a deep blue sky overhead—the Italian florists were spreading their many-colored perfumed wares on the stalls in Union Square. From Powell Street came the jangle of the cable car's bell as it crept up Nob Hill. The population's light-colored clothes added a note of gaiety and holiday high spirits as far as the banking district on Montgomery Street.

The pale, blond city of San Francisco, built like Rome on seven hills, undulates between the Pacific Ocean and the Bay. It is without any doubt the most seductive city in the United States. Its even climate, cosmopolitan population and superb location on one of the world's most beautiful waterways make it a particular favorite of sailors of all nations.

The news of the war in Europe was dying down by the time it reached San Francisco. But on this particular day, it made its presence felt through the sudden appearance of some sky-blue uniforms in the streets. They belonged to a group of French soldiers, natives of Tahiti, who were being sent home after three years of war and were now awaiting the uncertain departure of their ship. They were on their way to the White House, a hotel on Jackson Street, at the invitation of its proprietor, a Frenchman named Firmignac. The hotel's well-known restaurant was the meeting place for all Frenchmen in the San Francisco area.

Most of the Tahitians were either half-castes or Creole. There was Elie Juvetin, son of a Papeete printer, Edouard Thuret whose father was a notary, Maurice Langomazino and his brother Paul, who had just signed up with the United States Navy and was strutting proudly in his new uniform. They were immediately surrounded and questioned, their participation in the heroic defense of Verdun having crowned them with heroes' laurels.

One of the regular customers entered the bar, a big athletic man in his late fifties in an impeccable light gray suit. He went up to the group and, addressing Juvetin, said: "You are from Tahiti, I hear. I was there myself, over twenty-five years ago. How is Prince Hinoi? As jovial and friendly as ever, I've been told, and I'm sure just as large! Does Cape still have his store on the quay next to Sosthène Drollet's?"

"I suppose so, or at least that's the way it was when we left Tahiti over two years ago."

"Do you happen to know Hippolyte Mirey?"

"Mirey? You mean the old man who's the governor's cook?"

"That's the one. So he's had a nice promotion! He's one of my best friends, you know. When you see him, don't forget to tell him I'm coming to see him in Tahiti just as soon as I can."

The stranger then handed him an American-style business card on which was printed:

Eugène A. Degrave
First National Bank
Monterey, California

Juvetin took the card and looked at it casually, without registering surprise. To a young man not even born at the time of the *Niuroahiti* drama, the name meant nothing. A full generation separated the two men.

A few weeks later, Elie Juvetin met Mirey on the Papeete quays.

"Pori! We saw a *popaa* [European] in San Francisco who knows you well. He said he expected to come and see you soon."

"What is his name?" Mirey asked, intrigued.

"I don't remember. But wait a minute; I think I have his card in my wallet. Here."

Mirey took the card and suddenly started to sputter: "But ... but ... it isn't possible! It can't be! Rorique! Joseph Rorique!"

"What do you mean?" Juvetin was aghast. "He's one of the Roriques of your old story?"

"Yes." Mirey had turned pale and was trembling. "That's him. That's his real name. Eugène Degrave. Did he really say he was coming to see me in Tahiti? He's coming to kill me, you know."

This was an interesting turn of events, and Juvetin spread the story far and wide. For three days, people talked of little else, then it was forgotten. But for Mirey, the shock of seeing that name again had a profound effect on him. From then on, whenever the arrival of the monthly mailboat from San Francisco was relayed by semaphore from Mount Faiere, Mirey leapt into the bus serving the west coast of the island and hid out with a relative in Tautira, fifty-five miles from Papeete. There he waited to learn if anyone answering Eugène's description had arrived.

At the beginning, everybody including his wife teased him for what seemed to them a delusion. But as the months went by, and Mirey continued to flee to the other end of the island as soon as a ship was reported, his family became dismayed. They didn't like these periodic flights and held it against Elie Juvetin, especially when Mirey lost his job as the governor's cook after a fifteen-year tenure.

He began to ramble and gesture wildly as he talked to himself: "I know it, I can feel it. Death is coming from San Francisco."

So passed the year 1918.

In October, Mirey was hospitalized for a minor ailment. On November 12, Papeete celebrated the news of the Armistice and the end of the war.

Late in the afternoon of the 16th, the *Navua*, a freighter of the Union Steamship Company of New Zealand that plied between San Francisco and Auckland, arrived in port.

Doctor Le Strat of the port medical service examined its bill of health and found it clean. He was aware that a few cases of the "Spanish flu," which had ravaged Europe and parts of the United States, had turned up in California, but he hoped Polynesia would escape the scourge. There were three ailing sailors among the crew, one of them a Tahitian. The sick were taken off on Motu-Uta, the island in the port that served as quarantine.

But the *fetii*, the sailor's parents, demanded that he be turned over to them. A compromise was reached whereby he would be placed in isolation in the small hospital in Papeete. The sailor was carried on a stretcher to the hospital in a Ford truck.

On his arrival, he was left on the veranda while the orderlies went about their business. Mirey, who was convalescing, happened to wander by and, recognizing the sailor as a child he had known in Paea, went up to him. They shook hands and embraced even though the man looked very ill. The next day came the news that one of the men quarantined on Motu-Uta had died. On the 18th, the *Navua* was unable to sail; almost everyone on board was sick, including the captain.

On the 19th, the Tahitian sailor in the hospital died also. The doctors realized to their horror that the *Navua* had indeed brought the fatal virus. But for the time being, no one in Papeete seemed concerned. In the euphoria following the Armistice, a great banquet was being planned for the 23d, although many of the guests were already too sick to think of attending.

Mirey became feverish and took to his bed on the 22nd. The next day, he was in critical condition. On the 24th, he was dead.

Mirey had been right: for him, death did come from San Francisco.

In the register of deceased patients in the Papeete Hospital, there is the beautifully hand-written inscription: "Hippolyte Mirey, born September 25, 1856, in Paea [Tahiti], dead in Papeete on November 24, 1918."

The hand that wrote those words with such care could not have known that the name belonged to the first victim of an epidemic which, in three weeks, was to kill almost a third of Tahiti's population.

But Eugène Degrave was no more destined to end his days selling Malines lace than he was as a bank teller in California. In 1929, at the age of sixty-four, he launched an operation to prospect for amethysts in Colombia. He had found some American partners willing to risk large sums to back him and, in due course, he was able to deliver a sizable lot of amethysts to Bogotá. How did he come by them? Had he stolen them? Did he fail to observe the Colombian law controlling the exploitation of precious stones? Who knows?

His partner protested that Eugène was now trying to sell him amethysts he had already paid for in advance. Arrested as a thief, he was put in prison in Pamplona, and there, in conditions as strange as they were ill-documented, he died. His family was convinced he had been assassinated. And so, despite his full pardon, Eugène, like his brother Léonce, was fated to end his life in jail.

Captain Arnaud's metaphor of the ravished jewel box had achieved reality. There seems little doubt that the Rorique brothers were guilty of serious crimes, and that their virtues, like their vices, were of almost epic proportions. Given the dramatic scale of their lives and actions, it is sad that their saga had to come to such a lackluster end.